FIFTY UNIQUE LEGAL PATHS: HOW TO FIND THE RIGHT JOB

FIFTY UNIQUE LEGAL PATHS: HOW TO FIND THE RIGHT JOB

URSULA FURI-PERRY

Defending Liberty
Pursuing Justice

Library of Congress Cataloging-in-Publication Data

Furi-Perry, Ursula.
        Fifty unique legal paths / by Ursula Furi-Perry.
            p.   cm.
        Includes index.
        ISBN 978-1-59031-997-0
        1. Law—Vocational guidance—United States.   2. Lawyers—Employment—United States. 3. Practice of law—United States.
        I. Title.   II. Title: 50 unique legal paths.

    KF297.F87 2008
    340.023′73—dc22   2008042583

To my sons, Chase, Evan, and Roman,
And to other future JDs everywhere

TABLE OF CONTENTS

PREFACE

In the fall of 2007, I sat in historic Faneuil Hall in Boston waiting to be sworn in as a member of the Massachusetts Bar. One of our speakers prompted us new lawyers to think about the many different things we could do with our careers—ways in which we could make an impact and a difference. There were few limits to the career options that lay ahead.

Just months before, I had the privilege of giving a class graduation speech at the Massachusetts School of Law. "One of the best-kept secrets about the law degree is its versatility," I told the crowd. "Seldom has another degree inspired lists of 600 career tracks that can be followed upon its receipt. And as my life continues to require increased flexibility, I'm glad I opted for a degree that provides so much career choice and so many great legal paths that will allow us to impact the lives of countless people through our work."

Some say the JD is the new MBA—a resourceful higher degree that's useful in many fields and coveted by many employers, whether within or outside of the legal profession. The research, communication, and analytical skills that most law graduates possess make them great candidates for employment, making the JD a valuable degree.

While writing my first book, *50 Legal Careers for Nonlawyers* (ABA Publishing, 2008), I interviewed legal professionals about their careers and sought advice for those interested in the legal field. That was a book that gave readers a taste of many different areas of the legal field, making it different from most other legal career books, which tend to focus on one area. As I made countless new contacts and scheduled interviews for that book, many attorneys I talked with asked me the same question: Will you write a similar book for JDs?

So I did. Again, this book focuses on a variety of job options: fifty career tracks for law graduates. While I describe plenty of nonpracticing legal positions, I also address ten booming practice areas for attorneys, as well as some positions outside the legal field for which the JD degree is a natural fit. This is not a book just about nonattorney positions in the law or about shunning the law altogether. From banking to criminal justice, from education to ethics and compliance, the job market is ripe with opportunity for JDs—and this book describes those opportunities.

But most importantly, the book includes observations and advice from those who have made the JD their own: attorneys and law graduates who have carved out their own piece of the career pie. I'm a firm believer in putting firsthand insight into my books. Whether they are practicing law, working nonlegal jobs at law firms, or working outside the field, the people I interviewed for this book are all successful in their own right, leading fulfilling careers and staying involved in their profession.

And rather than just focusing on the destination, this book describes the journey—how each person got to a great position (sometimes rather unexpectedly) through a series of career changes and decisions. I hope their journeys inspire you to set out on a journey of your own toward the career that will prove to be your perfect fit!

ACKNOWLEDGMENTS

A heartfelt thank you to my editor Tim Brandhorst for all of his enthusiasm and belief in my books, and for working so hard to make them a success. A thanks to the entire ABA Publishing team—a pleasure to have worked together on two books so far.

Thank you to the accomplished, astute, and inspiring attorneys and JDs whom I had the privilege of interviewing and profiling. Your insight and advice for others is the essence of this book.

Thanks also to all of the trade organizations, bar associations, and other groups in the legal field whose management provided information and introduced me to their members to interview. You provide an invaluable service to legal professionals, and I hope readers will use the book's resources sections to help expand your memberships.

A final thank you to my husband, Tom, without whose support (not to mention inexhaustible help with child care) I couldn't have written this book.

CHAPTER 1

Growing Practice Areas for New JDs

With so many law books touting nonpracticing career opportunities outside the legal field, one might think law graduates are no longer looking to actually practice law! That is far from the truth. While some young lawyers complain of burnout and leave the practice, plenty of others are flocking to it still. Let's face it: A few people may go to law school knowing they want to work in an alternative legal career, but most law students are hoping to land a practicing legal position. In fact, in its survey entitled "After the JD: First Results of a National Study of Legal Careers," the NALP Foundation for Law Career Research and Education reports that nearly 70 percent of new JDs practice law in a private firm setting. And while most of the press about attrition and associate mobility suggests it's large law firms that are most likely to drive young associates away, the same NALP Foundation study reports that practicing attorneys with the highest income—generally those at large firms—are actually the least likely to move.

The point? Don't buy into the nonattorney legal career myth, and don't discount the practice of law. But do look beyond the obvious: High-profile practice areas such as litigation and business law often get the most press and the most attention, but they are far from your only options. Undoubtedly, some other practice areas are growing in popularity and demand for capable law graduates. For example, increased need for legal services by the aging population—like estate planning and administration—means more work for those who practice elder law; increased attention on environmental concerns translates into job opportunities in environmental and natural resources law; and increased globalization has spawned a myriad subspecialties in international law, such as international transactional work and international human rights.

Following are ten practice areas that are growing in popularity and opportunity—areas you may not have considered. This chapter was written with young attorneys in mind. So, many of the people who tell their stories are recent law graduates, sharing advice about identifying their interest in a particular practice area and getting started.

Environmental Law

Koalani Kaulukukui is only a few years out of law school, but she has already found her dream job as an associate at Earthjustice, a nonprofit law firm dedicated to the environment. Working in the firm's Honolulu office, Kaulukukui drafts legal documents on behalf of aggrieved plaintiffs, performs case investigations, and attends community meetings. She's been involved in a wide variety of cases, from cleaning up landfills on military bases to filing suit against the U.S. Navy for using sonar, which she says was killing whales.

Kaulukukui recently filed a water rights case on behalf of environmental groups in Maui, in an attempt to increase the minimum amount of water that needs to be kept in four streams in four valleys and enjoin sugar plantations from diverting the water from Hawaiian citizens. As part of her job, she identified and contacted water users to find out who had the right to use the streams' water and organized testimony by water users. She says she's developed a thick skin while working in environmental law: Though lots of people side with environmental groups and law firms like Kaulukukui's, others aren't so sympathetic, she says.

Environmental law jobs can be found in various sectors, explains Jay Tutchton, professor and director of the Environmental Law Clinic at the University of Denver School of Law. Though most jobs may be in public interest environmental law at small and large environmental groups, some environmental lawyers represent corporate clients or industries, while others work for the government. Learning each side's position is essential, Kaulukukui believes. "It's good to have a rounded experience," she says, "and important to understand where each side is coming from."

Those who represent environmental groups may file suits to protect endangered species, enforce environmental laws, and enjoin their violations. Government environmental lawyers at such agencies as the Environmental Protection Agency and its state counterparts work to stop, prosecute, and prevent environmental violations. Still others might represent plaintiffs injured by toxic materials or defendants who are responsible for those materials.

2

ENVIRONMENTAL AND NATURAL RESOURCES LAW: SOME SUBSPECIALTIES

The ABA Section of Environment, Energy, and Resources lists the following committees on its website:

Environmental Committees

- Agricultural Management
- Air Quality
- Climate Change, Sustainable Development, and Ecosystems
- Endangered Species
- Environmental Disclosure
- Environmental Enforcement and Crimes
- Environmental Justice, Special Committee on
- Environmental Litigation and Toxic Torts
- Environmental Transactions and Brownfields
- International Environmental Law
- Pesticides, Chemical Regulation, and Right-to-Know
- Site Remediation
- Smart Growth and Urban Policy
- State and Regional Environmental Cooperation
- Superfund and Natural Resource Damages Litigation
- Waste Management
- Water Quality and Wetlands

Energy and Resources Committees

- Energy and Environmental Finance, Special Committee on
- Energy and Natural Resources Litigation
- Energy Facilities and Siting
- Forest Resources
- Gas and Electricity Marketing
- Global Oil and Gas Exploration and Production
- Hydro Power
- International Energy and Resources Transactions
- Marine Resources
- Mining
- Native American Resources
- Petroleum Marketing
- Public Land and Resources
- Renewable Energy Resources

- Restructuring of the Electric Industry
- Water Resources

Cross Practice Committees and Task Forces

- Alternative Dispute Resolution
- Constitutional Law
- Environmental Impact Assessment
- Environmental Value and Ethics
- Ethics
- Homeland Security
- In-House Counsel
- Innovation, Management Systems, and Trading
- Science and Technology

Tutchton's clinic specializes in saving endangered species. His students often file actions to enforce laws that protect such species as the endangered jumping mouse or the prairie dog. Rather than taking on "flagship" endangered species—the ones that tend to make for cute calendars—Tutchton says he relishes representing species that generally don't get much attention, even snails and plants. "I kind of like accepting the long shots because they tend to have nowhere else to go," he says.

During law school, Tutchton completed a legal defense externship with the Sierra Club, which happened to be during the infamous Exxon-Valdez spill. "You felt like you were on the right side of the right issue," he says. As a professor, "a big part of what I do is to get students to pursue a career in this field," Tutchton says. "They go away recognizing that their [environmental lawyer] opponents are sane and should not be demonized."

Some of the field's greatest challenges can be attributed to the way environmental advocates are sometimes viewed by the public. "A lot of folks believe that environmentalists are very [much] against development; that we don't want progress," Kaulukukui says. As an example, she remembers a large sugar plantation that filed an intervenor against her firm, purporting itself to be a "proponent of change" and painting the environmental law firm as resistant to change. Yet "there's a way of working to move things forward without destroying what we have," Kaulukukui believes.

ENVIRONMENTAL LAW: BREAK-IN TIP

Though environmental law can be hard to break into, "there's more opportunity out there than one might think," says Kaulukukui, including positions in government, private law firms, and consulting. She began at the Office of Hawaiian Affairs, where she used her law degree to research and analyze issues. Kaulukukui says her experiences both in and after law school have shaped her career in environmental law. Government agencies are a good place to start, Kaulukukui believes, "a good place to get to know the players in the field and understand how the system works." If you can't find an opening in environmental law, consider taking on an internship to get your foot in the door.

For some, salaries might present a bar from entering the field—particularly in public interest environmental law. "If you're interested in a public interest career, you might look at a law school that has debt relief," Tutchton notes, or look for a loan repayment assistance program. "Because of the nature of these small environmental groups, jobs are eclectic and sometimes term limited," Tutchton explains; some grants and funds, for example, may limit employment to a year.

The environmental law field needs lots of committed manpower, Tutchton says. He compares it with emergency room triage. "There is so much work to be done," he says. "Because of the overwhelming need and scarce resources, we can't take every case."

Tutchton believes the environmental law movement is one of the more important social movements in a couple of generations and says the best part of his job is explaining to kids what he does. "I like my clients; I like the issues that I'm working on; [and] I feel good at the end of the day," he says. "[Law graduates] have to remember that a law degree is power. Use that power for good. Remember why you went to law school and act on that belief."

International Law

Most people think of international law in the "public" sense: the relations between different nations. But international law isn't just about diplomacy—this specialty encompasses a whole slew of subspecialties, including international business law, international transactional law, and international human rights. In fact, with increased globalization and ever-developing connections between people from different nations, international law can affect pretty much all lawyers at some point in their legal careers.

As an associate focusing on international arbitration matters at Milbank Tweed Hadley McCloy, LLP, in Washington, D.C., Frederic Sourgens represents parties in international disputes at arbitration proceedings and negotiates on their behalf. He says he sometimes marvels at the figures he handles, particularly as a practitioner who's only a few years out of law school—Sourgens's first arbitration centered around a $36 billion contract, and he estimates that his lowest deal was worth about $40 million.

Recent law grad Anna Andreeva also works on deals worth millions of dollars as an associate focusing on international and commercial transactional law at White & Case, LLP, in Miami. Andreeva often handles bank finance work with foreign banks, lenders, and borrowers, as well as aircraft finance work with foreign airlines. As part of her job, she drafts agreements and loans, contacts parties for signature, and coordinates all documents to make sure deals are ready for closing.

"The most difficult thing is learning to coordinate," says Andreeva. Because international transactional attorneys often have to take charge of every party's documents, signatures, and comments, Andreeva says the job can make one feel like a ringmaster. "You have to work across time zones," she says, which means scheduling in advance to meet everyone's needs and accounting for schedule changes as needed.

Sourgens says it helps to have something of a general focus in international arbitration, such as understanding basic contract and transactional law. Still, research skills and some familiarity with finding international laws are necessary. For example, says Sourgens, "You have to have the curiosity to figure out, 'How does this work in Algerian law?'" Sourgens notes that most of his work centers on comparative law; he also says that public international concepts are sometimes important in his field, even where the transactions are private, as some contracts may be based on international treaties or involve a public or state-owned entity.

International law isn't just a practice area—it is a field that plays an increasingly important part of the practice of law in general. "It's important on even a most basic level," says Sourgens, noting that every lawyer might encounter an international issue one day, even those who practice in the most local environments. With increased globalization, firms are expanding to other countries and relying on their lawyers to be able to understand and research international issues.

Though not always essential, language skills can be helpful for those working in the field. Andreeva says her fluency in Russian and Spanish

INTERNATIONAL LAW: SOME SUBSPECIALTIES

- Public international law
- International human rights law
- International transactional law
- International business law
- International arbitration
- Comparative law
- International criminal law
- International tax law
- International antitrust law
- Customs law/national security law
- International investments and development
- International environmental law

made her not just more marketable but also more trustworthy to clients who are more comfortable handling negotiations and deals in their own language. Sourgens also speaks several languages.

INTERNATIONAL LAW: BREAK-IN TIP

Sourgens emphasizes the value of being published in the international law field. "One of the better ways to be successful is to try to take a few courses, show an interest, and start publishing," he says. He recommends that interested attorneys tackle a narrow question in international or comparative law that hasn't gotten much press, research it, and write about it. Sourgens also notes that when it comes to international law, networking takes on quite a different look from other fields—after all, it's not always feasible for new attorneys to attend conferences half a world away, which can be quite expensive. Sourgens recommends making good use of technology in networking. He says listservs, online journals, and even conference calls can be invaluable in keeping up with the rest of the profession.

As might be expected, such a specialized field isn't easy to break into. Sourgens says those who are interested in international law should not be afraid to approach firms that practice in this area and market their skills. "Get specific about what part of international law is interesting, research who does it, and really start to approach people," he advises. Sourgens adds that it took him quite a few calls and emails to land interviews. "Keep trying," he says. "I've seen quite a few people have an incredibly frustrating time."

For young lawyers working in the field, international law can present a fulfilling career. "It gives me the opportunity to learn and to grow professionally," says Andreeva.

Intellectual Property

Jason Nickla is another recent law graduate who's already making strides in his field—in fact, he currently fills two positions at Cardinal Intellectual Property in Evanston, Illinois, serving as both patent attorney and project manager. In the latter position, Nickla is contracted to perform patent searches on behalf of private clients, while another attorney handles searches on behalf of the U.S. Patent and Trademarks Office (PTO). Nickla prepares search reports, reviews them with the clients, and serves as the point of contact for clients on technical and legal questions.

Nickla has an undergraduate science degree and specializes in biosciences. He worked for a trucking company on licensing matters after college, and although he initially contemplated getting his Ph.D. in pharmacology, he ultimately decided to go to law school after getting bombarded with questions about licensing deals. Law school "was going to enable me to see a lot of different areas of the sciences rather than being pigeon-holed," Nickla explains. Working as a patent attorney right out of law school, Nickla says he enjoyed exposure to electrical and mechanical patent applications, not just those dealing with biology.

As a patent attorney, Nickla handled applications on behalf of inventors who sought patents and represented them in front of the U.S. PTO. Among his job responsibilities were reviewing and drafting the application, corresponding with clients and the PTO, and responding to official PTO office actions. Nickla's job was in patent prosecution, taking an application from start to finish and ensuring that inventors get their patents and proper protection from infringement. But plenty of other opportunities exist in intellectual property. For example, some attorneys focus on getting authors copyrights, while others litigate patent, trademark, or copyright infringements, and still others focus on licensing and related contracts.

INTELLECTUAL PROPERTY LAW: SOME SUBSPECIALTIES

- Patent prosecution
- Patent litigation
- Trademark law
- Copyright law
- Licensing and management
- Information technology
- Trade secrets

Nickla says that while a science background is necessary in order to represent patent applicants in front of the U.S. PTO—including passing the Patent Bar—the same degree isn't necessary for those who seek to work in patent litigation, trademarks, copyrights, or other subspecialties in intellectual property law. "There are people who don't have the technical [background] and do the litigation side," Nickla explains. A law license is typically necessary to represent clients, though the U.S. Patent and Trademarks Office allows nonattorney patent agents to prosecute patent applications as well.

Nickla says the most challenging part of his current position is juggling many different matters; he says he is constantly interrupted and can't block out hours to work on one particular project—unlike in his prior work as a patent attorney, when he could more easily shut his office door to work on a patent application. As an attorney, Nickla enjoyed seeing new ideas and inventions and taking them through the patent process from start to finish. "You feel like you have a little inside scoop on what's new in technology," he says.

INTELLECTUAL PROPERTY LAW: BREAK-IN TIP

In such a specialized field as intellectual property, it can be helpful to have some narrowly focused continuing education. After completing his law degree, Nickla went back for his LL.M. in intellectual property law—he says he wanted to get a more focused perspective in his specialty and also thought he would make valuable connections to help him find a job upon graduating. Nickla swears by the value of networking in general; he found his current position while talking with one of the company's searchers at a professional association event.

It's hard to tell which degree is more valuable in the patent field, and Nickla believes both his technical background and his JD give him credibility with clients. And while a technical or scientific degree is essential to understanding the makeup of each patent application, the JD can be invaluable, like when deciding if something is privileged or confidential, Nickla says.

The fact that he ended up in his current positions—particularly the narrow niche of being a patent search project manager—hasn't surprised Nickla, even though some of his current projects have proven to be outside his comfort zone. "Sometimes, you're forced to forge your own path," he says. "You have to be flexible, be willing to do what you may not be comfortable with, and you might just surprise yourself and enjoy it."

Science and Technology Law

If you like having your finger on the pulse and have a background or interest in science or technology, your law degree affords you plenty of options. An emerging and exciting field, science and technology law encompasses the legal side of several subfields, including computers and information technology, biosciences, engineering, biotechnology, and scientific evidence, to name just a few.

The dot-com bust took Shiv Naimpally to law school. Working in technology marketing with a computer science background, Naimpally was laid off in 2002 after a seventeen-year career in computer science and decided to go to graduate school. He decided against an MBA, which he found increasingly common in his field; rather, after learning about opportunities in intellectual property law and science and technology law, Naimpally went to law school. "When I discovered that I could actually use my [science] background to my advantage, then law school became a possibility," he says.

Now, the recent grad works as a patent associate at Toler Schaffer in Austin, Texas, filing and prosecuting patent applications on behalf of inventors. Naimpally says he initially considered becoming a patent agent: a nonattorney professional who may represent patent applicants in front of the U.S. Patent and Trademarks Office. After doing some contract work for law firms writing patent applications, Naimpally opted to get his law degree.

Naimpally says he enjoys working in science and technology law, particularly because the field is emerging and growing in so many ways. Science and technology law touches on many innovative concepts and ideas, Naimpally says. Government regulations by administrative agencies such as the Food and Drug Administration or the Federal Trade

SCIENCE AND TECHNOLOGY LAW: SOME SUBSPECIALTIES

The ABA Section of Science and Technology Law lists the following divisions and committees on its website:

E-Commerce and IT Division

- Blogs and User-Generated Content on the Internet
- E-Commerce Payment
- Electronic Filing
- E-Privacy Law
- Information Security
- Latin American E-Commerce
- Open Source
- Privacy and Computer Crime
- Technical Standardization
- Telecommunications and Mass Media
- Virtual Worlds and Multiuser Online Games
- Voice-over-Internet Protocol
- Wi-Fi

Life and Physical Sciences Division

- Animal Research
- Behavioral Sciences
- Biotechnology
- Nanotechnology Law
- Public Health, Environmental Law, and Preparedness
- Rights and Responsibilities of Scientists
- Scientific Evidence

Interdisciplinary Division

- Artificial Intelligence and Robotics
- Future of Evidence
- Homeland Security
- International Policy
- Museum Law
- Space Law

Commission; e-commerce and First Amendment issues on the Internet; family law questions dealing with frozen embryos and sperm donations; medical privacy laws in an age of "superbugs"; and peer-to-peer technology questions are just some of the ones that Naimpally mentions.

SCIENCE AND TECHNOLOGY LAW: BREAK-IN TIP

This is one field that requires not only legal knowledge but also substantive knowledge and an understanding of the underlying subject matter: science and technology. Many lawyers enter the field with some academic or employment background in the sciences; in fact, the U.S. PTO requires a science degree to represent clients in patent prosecution. Even if you don't plan to represent clients in front of the PTO, Naimpally recommends continuing education in the sciences to help you figure out which subspecialties may interest you and to understand the processes and "lingo" of the field you choose. He also recommends joining professional associations as early on in your career as possible—Naimpally, for instance, served as the student liaison for the ABA Section of Science and Technology Law.

Because science and technology law continues to evolve, those practicing it have to be able to learn quickly and be ready for constant change, Naimpally says. "There are always new and interesting challenges coming up," he says. "Science and technology touch people in many different ways."

Entertainment Law

Some describe entertainment law as a fusion of intellectual property and business law. Representing artists, writers, actors, musicians, and other figures in the industry, entertainment lawyers serve as key people in the marriage of creativity and legal issues.

Recent law grad Daliah Saper found out about entertainment law opportunities as a law student, at a career event held by her law school. Though she knew she wanted to do something creative and had already joined the Intellectual Property Law Students Association, it wasn't until she attended a talk by the general counsel of *Playboy* magazine that Saper instantly knew she was interested in the fast-paced field of entertainment law. In fact, she was so interested that she asked *Playboy* for an internship—and kept asking, despite being told there were no openings, until a semester-long internship position was created by the magazine just for her.

After graduation, Saper worked for a sole practitioner, did some public relations work for a fashion design company, and finally started her own firm—a move that she says was challenging, but definitely worth it. Though Saper had no clients to take with her at the time, she says she also didn't have anything to lose, as she wasn't leaving a high salary or a satisfying practice. As founder of the Saper Law Firm in Chicago, she says she enjoys a niche in working with up-and-coming musicians and artists.

ENTERTAINMENT LAW: SOME SUBSPECIALTIES

The ABA Forum Committee on the Entertainment and Sports Industries lists subspecialties in the following divisions:

- Merchandising and Licensing
- Motion Pictures, Television, Cable, and Radio
- Music and Personal Appearances
- Legitimate Theater and Performing Arts
- Sports
- Literary Publishing
- Interactive Media and New Technologies
- Arts and Museum

Though entertainment law may seem like all fun and games, Saper says, "people should know what they're getting into. [Entertainment law] is very business-heavy and industry-specific." Also, "people should go into it knowing that all entertainment law isn't the same," Saper says. While a broad overview of the field and an understanding of how the industry works are essential, Saper says most entertainment lawyers specialize in a subset of the field—depending on what the majority of their clients are doing, where they are located, and what opportunities the field affords.

If show business is all about whom you know, then entertainment law likewise requires a mastery of networking, perhaps even more so than many other practice areas, as this is such a highly specialized field. "I had to build my own network," Saper says, adding that the reason she is able to have her own firm so soon after graduating law school is because she has people she can trust and call when she has a question or issue with which she needs help. Likewise, she says she serves as a resource for others who need her help and expertise. How to get connected? "A great way is to start with some commonality," Saper says. She recalls her first contact with one of the people who would become a mentor: She

13

ENTERTAINMENT LAW: BREAK-IN TIP

"Look for places that are unconventional," says Saper, such as small production companies and up-and-coming people in the industry who need legal help but can't afford to hire a big firm. Saper says grads who are just starting out should be willing to work for free if necessary; she also says they should keep looking for opportunities. She points out that she got her internship at *Playboy* even after she was repeatedly turned down and told there were no openings at the time; because she kept pursuing the opportunity, that opportunity created itself for her. The moral of the story? JDs interested in entertainment law—or any particular area, for that matter—should not give up looking for a chance to learn about and break into the field.

---

emailed him and used the fact that they attended the same law school as common ground to break the ice. He agreed to have coffee with her and talk, and he soon became her friend and mentor.

Saper also says that recent graduates should try on practice areas for size before deciding on one. She believes that practical experience—through clinics and internships, for example—is more important than coursework and says that it took her internship at *Playboy* to reinforce that entertainment law was the right field for her.

Health Law

From overseeing hospital regulations to bringing suits against negligent medical professionals, from enforcing privacy laws in health care settings to monitoring doctors' conduct, health law attorneys work in a unique fusion of law and medicine. With an increased focus on health issues and a growing aging population, health law is an evolving career option and a viable field for new attorneys with the right skill set and qualifications.

During law school, Luz Carrion worked as a paralegal at the Massachusetts Board of Registration in Medicine in Boston. After graduating, she held a clerkship and worked as an assistant district attorney but kept in touch with her old employer. Just two years out of law school, Carrion was hired as the board's complaint counsel when the position opened up. She works with the board's enforcement division, receiving and investigating complaints against doctors and pursuing disciplinary actions where necessary. Once her investigation is complete, Carrion determines what violations, if any, have been committed, and presents her findings to the complaint committee with a recommendation for actions to be taken.

Though most cases settle for sanctions, Carrion also represents the board at formal administrative hearings against doctors who choose to fight the complaints; there, she calls witnesses and presents evidence on behalf of the board. Finally, she assists the board with case disposition. She says the complaints she has seen run the gamut: sexual misconduct, fraud, licensing matters, impairment on the job, and disruptive behavior are some examples.

HEALTH LAW: SOME SUBSPECIALTIES

The American Health Lawyers Association (AHLA) lists the following practice groups on its website:

- Antitrust
- Fraud and Abuse, Self-Referrals, and False Claims
- Health Information and Technology
- Healthcare Liability and Litigation
- HMOs and Health Plans
- Hospitals and Health Systems
- In-house Counsel
- Labor and Employment
- Life Sciences
- Long-Term Care
- Medical Staff, Credentialing, and Peer Review
- Physician Organizations
- Regulation, Accreditation, and Payment

Carrion says one of the greatest challenges in her position, as in so many other practice areas, is balancing many cases at the same time. "We have a heavy case load," she says. In some instances, it can also be tough to get the doctor or hospital that is involved to cooperate. Although Carrion usually deals with cooperative professionals, she says she's had to go to court to enforce subpoenas in the past. Those who are interested in health law must be able to multitask and prioritize, she says, recognizing when a case is important enough to be moved up on the to-do list. "When you have a serious case [where] you think the public is at risk, that takes priority," she explains.

For Carrion, the most rewarding part of her position is playing a part in enforcing the law and making sure the medical field is safe. "We want to ensure that patients are safe and the best medical care is rendered," she says. "I think we do make a difference in the quality of care." And in some cases—like when prosecuting doctors for fraud—Carrion says she also feels that she helps protect the medical profession's integrity.

HEALTH LAW: BREAK-IN TIP

Though a background in medicine or the health care field can be immensely helpful in a career in health law, it is not generally essential. In some positions, however, having medical experience is clearly important. For instance, those with a health care background can find careers in consulting or expert witness opportunities.

The JD degree has been important in Carrion's position, particularly when it comes to issue spotting and research skills. "You're not going to have all the answers," Carrion explains. Most attorneys—especially those who have no medical or health care background—wouldn't know the answers to medical questions and issues, but the research skills they learned in law school allow them to look up those answers as needed. Carrion cites the standard of care as one big issue that keeps changing over time, challenging her research skills. Carrion says she enjoys the research component of her job and the intellectual curiosity it creates. "What I like about it is that I'm always learning," she says.

Elder Law

The growing aging population doesn't just need legal advice from attorneys who focus on health law—elder law is becoming a growing practice area as well. The field of elder law encompasses many subspecialties that focus on serving the aging population, including estate planning and administration, nursing home litigation, and grandparents' rights.

"It's a specialty that's defined by the client, not by the law, so it's very horizontal," explains Craig Reaves, an elder law attorney at the Reaves Law Firm in Kansas City, Missouri, and president of the National Academy of Elder Law Attorneys. Reaves says he was always interested in estate planning and began focusing on elder law and disability law after he was approached by a family with a child who had Down Syndrome.

Reaves set up a special needs trust for the child. "That taught me the Medicaid system and the SSI system, and as my clients began aging or my clients' parents had issues, [I began practicing] elder law," he says.

Reaves says most people tend to come into elder law from one of two subspecialties: traditional estate planning or providing legal aid to the

---

ELDER LAW: SOME SUBSPECIALTIES

The National Academy of Elder Law Attorneys lists the following subspecialties on its website:

- Preservation/transfer of assets seeking to avoid spousal impoverishment when a spouse enters a nursing home
- Medicaid
- Medicare claims and appeals
- Social security and disability claims and appeals
- Supplemental and long term health insurance issues.
- Disability planning, including use of durable powers of attorney, living trusts, "living wills," for financial management and health care decisions, and other means of delegating management and decision-making to another in case of incompetency or incapacity
- Conservatorships and guardianships
- Estate planning, including planning for the management of one's estate during life and its disposition on death through the use of trusts, wills, and other planning documents
- Probate
- Administration and management of trusts and estates
- Long-term care placements in nursing home and life care communities
- Nursing home issues, including questions of patients' rights and nursing home quality
- Elder abuse and fraud recovery cases
- Housing issues, including discrimination and home equity conversions
- Age discrimination in employment
- Retirement, including public and private retirement benefits, survivor benefits and pension benefits
- Health law
- Mental health law

---

elderly. The majority of attorneys tend to specialize in a subset of elder law, such as probate or nursing home litigation, and Reaves says most tend to work in small firm or solo practitioner settings. Reaves says his estate planning practice focuses on protecting clients' assets; he also does guardianship work and probate work.

Reaves also did something uncommon: He set out as a sole practitioner immediately after becoming an attorney—and within two years of going solo, he had hired his first employees. Though he later merged with two other small firms, Reaves returned to solo practice in 1988.

Reaves notes that those interested in estate planning must have exceptional people skills and communication skills. "This is a very touchy-feely, emotional kind of practice," says Reaves. "You need to have compassion; you need to have the ability to communicate at different levels," from the client with dementia to the client's working professional children. "Sometimes you're dealing with people who are irrational," says Reaves. "They may be the one who has a disability [or] they may be dealing with extreme grief," like clients in need of a special needs trust after a serious injury who have had their lives changed in an instant. "They can lash out in many ways; they can not make good decisions [at times]," Reaves explains.

Drafting skills are also important, as is being able to take the client's needs and wishes and translate them into something that works well legally. "People come in with an idea . . . and you help [them] flesh out what their concept is," Reaves explains, "[to be sure] it's understandable, does what they wanted, and complies with the law."

ELDER LAW: BREAK-IN TIP

Reaves recommends talking with—and maybe even shadowing—an elder law attorney to see if the field is the right fit. He says that while elder law is becoming "more and more written," it is still an emerging field and most of it is learned not from courses and books but through practice and observing people.

In elder law, "you get paid a lot in good deed points," Reaves says. The most rewarding part is "being able to take very overwhelming, complicated circumstances that people are thrust into" and turn them around. "To take a person from that and get them through the process . . . you become glued emotionally with them and they are usually so appreciative."

Immigration Law

Though some think of immigration law as a field fraught only with administrative practice and paper-pushing, it also involves a lot of human drama. From assisting refugees and immigrants seeking asylum to representing families separated by borders, immigration lawyers help their clients through emotional and life-changing events, explains Jeff Joseph, partner in the Joseph Law Firm in Aurora, Colorado. Joseph says some of his clients have stayed with him for decades: Take an immigrant coming in on a student visa, for example, who is later sponsored by an employer or spouse to become a legal permanent resident, then later applies for citizenship, and then in turn sponsors immediate family members back home to come live in the United States. The immigration lawyer might see the client through all of these different events through the years.

Still, there's undoubtedly a lot of paperwork in immigration law, Joseph says. There's also a lot of research and keeping up with regulations, some of which change daily. Joseph says he spends the first hour of his morning just catching up on what happened the previous day.

There are three main subspecialties in which most immigration attorneys practice, explains Carlina Tapia-Ruano, partner at Tapia-Ruano & Gunn, PC, in Chicago and immediate past national president of the American Immigration Lawyers Association (AILA). Those who practice immigrant defense represent foreign nationals before the immigration office or immigration courts, she says; those who practice family immigration assist individuals who are trying to obtain immigration benefits based on family relationships; and those who practice business immigration represent clients in employment-based or investment-based matters. Tapia-Ruano says most attorneys focus on one subspecialty. "They're very different from one another," she says, and each "requires that you keep up with drastic changes."

IMMIGRATION LAW: SOME SUBSPECIALTIES

- Business and employment-based immigration
- Relative-based or family immigration
- Asylum and refugee representation
- Removal representation
- Government work: enforcement, application processing, or agency representation in court

"Behind every piece of paper is a story," says Joseph. "You really get exposed to people from different backgrounds." Joseph says it's a misconception that immigration law entails representing only Spanish-speaking clients from south of the border; he says he represents clients from many cultural and social backgrounds, from millionaire foreign investors to asylees who have nothing but the clothes on their backs. Being exposed to a multicultural environment is rewarding, but can also present challenges. "You have to learn to adapt to the way that people handle professional affairs," Joseph explains; in some cases, for example, immigrants may be distrustful of attorneys, while others revere attorneys in their home countries. Joseph says it can take him years just to get the client's full story, particularly in cases of political asylum fraught with abuse. "A lot of what we do really intersects with social work," he says. "You have to have compassion and be able to convey that to an adjudicator who sees thousands of [cases] per year." Tapia-Ruano says some of her most rewarding cases come from people she's represented in deportation proceedings, then later assisted with citizenship petitions—helping them to become fully contributing members of U.S. society.

Joseph recalls one particular case that touched his heart. He represented a school-age Iraqi boy who had approached American soldiers while brandishing a weapon, urging them to take him into custody. Once the soldiers did, the boy divulged a list of names of terrorists—one of them the boy's own father, a Republican Guard, who had been pressuring the boy to practice violence against Americans. The boy became an immediate walking death threat, Joseph says, and the rest of his family was murdered. The boy, however, was brought to the United States and successfully represented by Joseph in his application for political asylum. At his asylum interview, the government interviewee—a former military officer—even saluted the boy.

The skill set required of immigration lawyers depends largely on the subspecialty they choose, says Tapia-Ruano. For example, she says those representing immigrants in court should be articulate and quick on their feet; business immigration lawyers have to be proficient at paperwork; family immigration specialists must have great people skills. All immigration lawyers have to be obsessive about detail, Joseph says, as there are many deadlines and intricacies involved. Also, "you have to be prepared for defeat," Joseph says. "The odds are against you [and] it's a challenge to try to work through the system." Knowledge of a second language isn't necessarily required, but can be very helpful.

Tapia-Ruano says her work is fulfilling because "I am always defending or representing someone who's trying to improve their lives, and

---

IMMIGRATION LAW: BREAK-IN TIP

"Take on some pro bono cases," recommends Joseph. "Immigration law really lends itself to pro bono work." Joseph says that because immigration law is subject to constant change, it is a field where new attorneys can blossom as soon as they graduate. "Unlike other areas of law that are governed by precedent, immigration law reinvents itself almost on a daily basis," he explains, so new attorneys are "starting out on the same footing" as those who have been working in the field for years—in fact, those with great research skills may fare even better. Though the field can present many opportunities for sole practitioners, Tapia-Ruano and Joseph both recommend that new attorneys get some experience working in immigration law before they strike out on their own. Joseph started his law firm just about a year and a half after graduating, but he says he got valuable experience working for another immigration law firm beforehand. Internships in the field won't give a perfectly accurate picture of what it's like to practice immigration law, Tapia-Ruano and Joseph both add, as internships tend to focus on clinical experience rather than working with forms, which still makes up the brunt of the immigration attorney's work.

---

through that process, they benefit the U.S." Constant changes also make the practice interesting. "I feel like we're on the cusp of really exciting changes on the policy level," Joseph says. "To be practicing law on the cusp of political change is very exciting."

Labor and Employment Law

John Fox describes labor and employment law as a field that "always has an emotional or real side to it and doesn't involve any dry aspects." Partner in the Palo Alto, California, office of Manatt, Phelps & Phillips, LLP, Fox handles cases involving trade secrets, wage-hour and discrimination class actions, wrongful termination, corporate investigations, and the use of statistics in employment matters. He also advises business clients on employment practices and strategy.

Litigating cases and advising clients make up most employment lawyers' work. Fox believes that a 70-30 split between litigation and legal advice is ideal for employment and labor lawyers. "You really cannot give competent advice until you've tried cases and see the kind of pressure that can be put on the company policy," he says. Fox also says that litigation forces him to be crisp: Under the pressure of litigation, "you need to know exactly what the line is between what the law permits and what the law forbids," he says, unlike when advice is being given to the client only, without opposing counsel in the forefront.

Fox says it's difficult to truly specialize in one particular subset of employment law, as each case or client policy is likely to involve many different rules or areas of law. Fox says he sees people specialize in traditional labor law as opposed to employment law, as the former, he says, has gotten highly technical.

LABOR AND EMPLOYMENT LAW: SOME SUBSPECIALTIES

The ABA Section of Labor and Employment Law lists the following standing committees:

- ADR [Alternative Dispute Resolution] in Labor and Employment Law
- Development of the Law under the NLRA [National Labor Relations Act]
- Employee Benefits
- Employment Rights and Responsibilities
- Equal Employment Opportunity
- Ethics and Professional Responsibility
- Federal Labor Standards Legislation
- Federal Legislative Developments
- Federal Service Labor and Employment Law
- Immigration Law
- International Labor Law
- Occupational Safety and Health Law
- Practice and Procedure under the NLRA
- Railway and Airline Labor Law
- State and Local Government Bargaining and Employment Law
- Technology in the Practice and Workplace
- Union Administration and Procedure
- Workers' Compensation

The field is "definitely growing and definitely satisfying, but it's also definitely changing," says Fox. Decades ago, he recalls being able to read a short policy as research in most matters; now, Fox says his associates "need a library card" and deal with thousands of pages of research, case law, and policies.

But employment law isn't just about knowing the law and knowing where to find it. Behind each company policy or case are human issues, says Fox. In fact, lawyers can make a difference in the lives of employers and employees alike. Fox recalls one case of bad advice given to a small employer (Fox's client) who had outsourced human resources to a third party provider. The provider advised the client to fire a young employee who had bladder cancer—and the client fired the man on the day he was going in for his first round of chemotherapy. "I really liked the plaintiff," said Fox; so did the company, as the employee had a good record. At a deposition, he took his CEO client aside and suggested that the company offer him reinstatement; they did, and the employee accepted. In the end, the client settled for attorneys' fees, saving money. "A lot of times, clients are well intentioned but so lost . . . that they just don't know how to proceed," explains Fox. "We can bring a lot of organization to the company and better thinking to the matter."

LABOR AND EMPLOYMENT LAW: BREAK-IN TIP

Fox says labor and employment law is a technical field, and not one that is easy to "fluidly step into." Fox recommends that those interested in the field "test it out," whether by clerking at a boutique labor and employment firm or by asking for labor and employment assignments at a large firm. Most importantly, if you're just starting out "it's a big mistake for people to say 'this is what I'm going to do for the rest of my life,'" says Fox, as it would be with any other practice area or specialty. Fox says he "fell into" the field: He worked as a reporter after law school, writing and editing legal digests, and began helping out a sole practitioner who specialized in labor law down the hall from his office. Soon, Fox was offered a job as a labor lawyer and accepted, and followed along when the lawyers' practice was acquired by a large firm. "The key is finding what you like to do," says Fox, and following one's interests while keeping an open mind to the big picture and other fields.

In labor and employment law, "there is a lot of business because everybody has employees," says Fox. "There is a lot of work to be done and a lot of opportunity."

Administrative Law

The field of administrative law encompasses many subspecialties, from banking regulatory practice to homeland security, from aviation and transportation law to health regulatory practice. Administrative lawyers work with the laws of executive agencies—federal and state—and explore how those agencies regulate the industry in which an attorney works, explains banking attorney Charlotte Bahin.

As a partner at Locke Lord Bissell & Liddell, LLP, in Washington, D.C., Bahin is building up the firm's banking practice. She has worked in banking law since before going to law school, working as a paralegal in a firm's financial services practice while attending law school at night. For sixteen years after graduating law school, Bahin served as an attorney for a trade organization representing a segment of the banking industry—there, she fielded legal and regulatory questions from people in the industry who sought her help. She then transitioned back into the law firm world when she was asked to start up her firm's new financial services practice.

Bahin says there are many different ways to define regulatory practice. "There's a piece that looks at what agencies are doing, what the regulations are, what powers the bank has and how those powers are being interpreted, and how banks can expand their powers," she says. As part of her practice, Bahin keeps up with banking law developments and looks at how those developments will affect the industry. She also represents some clients (banks) on deals, and answers other attorneys' questions about narrow topics in banking law.

One great challenge in administrative law lies in keeping track of every entity or agency that has a say in the industry in which a lawyer works. For example, Bahin explains that in banking, there are four primary federal regulators, another six to ten tangential federal regulators, plus at least one regulatory body in each state. Dealing with that many different sources of legal authority can be challenging. "It's not necessarily hard, but it's not the type of thing [where] you can just say 'I can figure it out on my own,'" says Bahin. As a partner building a practice from the ground up, Bahin adds that much of her current challenges come from finding clients.

Bahin recommends that those interested in administrative law start at a firm with an already established practice to learn the ropes. Though Bahin has known people who worked at banks before they went to law school and then became banking regulatory attorneys, she believes most people start out in the field as associates who are given banking responsibilities.

ADMINISTRATIVE LAW: SOME SUBSPECIALTIES

The ABA Section of Administrative Law and Regulatory Practice lists the following government functions committees:

- Agriculture
- Antitrust and Trade Regulation
- Banking and Financial Services
- Benefits
- Beverage Alcohol Practice
- Communications
- Consumer Products Regulation
- Criminal Process
- Education
- Elections
- Energy
- Environmental and Natural Resources Regulation
- Food and Drug
- Government Personnel
- Health and Human Services
- Homeland Security and National Defense
- Housing and Urban Development
- Immigration and Naturalization
- Insurance
- Intellectual Property
- International Law
- International Trade and Customs
- Labor and Employment Law
- Ombuds
- Postal Matters
- Securities, Commodities, and Exchanges
- Transportation
- Treasury, Revenue, and Tax
- Veterans Affairs

Bahin says transitioning from a large law firm—where she had hundreds of people to whom she could turn with questions—to a small trade organization was challenging, and she had to learn quickly how to figure out answers on her own. Her transition back into the law firm world has proven equally challenging, but for different reasons: She now deals with a wide-open job description and is responsible for ensuring that all of the work gets done.

ADMINISTRATIVE LAW: BREAK-IN TIP

If you're interested in administrative law, consider learning about several subspecialties in the field—you'll not only discover some career options but also develop a broader knowledge base. Because administrative law deals with many angles and questions, "it's very important to have a broad base [of knowledge] from which to draw," Bahin says. "If the person is fresh out of law school, they should try to get some exposure to the different areas and issues that banks work with," she says. "If it's somebody who's looking around for another type of law . . . I'd say [attend] CLE courses, maybe even try a project." Still in law school? The ABA Section of Administrative Law and Regulatory Practice—like many other sections and committees—offers a law student membership, with access to periodicals, CLE, and networking opportunities.

Bahin says her work in banking law has proven rewarding. "When I worked for the trade organization, there were times when I felt like what I did really made a difference," she says, like when working with a bank on a newly proposed regulation and pinpointing why the regulation might or might not make sense. Administrative law judge positions are also available to JDs. Administrative law judges preside over hearings in various subspecialties, including social security and disability cases and cases involving veterans' benefits. And of course, government agencies also hire administrative lawyers—see Chapter 3 for more detail.

Administrative law requires a solid understanding of basic civics and how the government works, Bahin says. "You have to be able to look at an agency and see how it interacts with the industry," she says, understanding such questions as why a national bank has to pay attention to what the OCC says, or why a national airline has to abide by FAA regulations. Much of administrative law entails "being able to look at the rules and think about how they apply," Bahin says, and "understanding the broader context of the regulatory world." For those tasks, a legal education is invaluable.

THERE'S MORE ON THE WEB!
Career Resources for This Chapter

Environmental Law

ABA Section of Environment, Energy, and Resources, http://www.abanet.org/environ/
Natural Resources and Environment, quarterly trade journal published by the ABA Section, http://www.abanet.org/environ/pubs/nre/

International Law

The American Society of International Law (ASIL), http://www.asil.org/index.html
The ASIL Guide to Electronic Resources in International Law, http://www.asil.org/resource/home.htm
International Bar Association (IBA), http://www.ibanet.org/
The Center for International Legal Studies, http://www.cils.net/
ABA Section of International Law, http://www.abanet.org/intlaw/home.html
International Bar News, trade journal published by the IBA (in addition to eight other IBA journals), http://www.ibanet.org/publications/international_bar_news.cfm
International Lawyer, quarterly trade journal published by the ABA Section, http://www.abanet.org/intlaw/pubs/home.html

Intellectual Property Law

American Intellectual Property Law Association (AIPLA), http://www.aipla.org/
ABA Section of Intellectual Property Law, http://www.abanet.org/intelprop/home.html
American Intellectual Property Law Association Quarterly Journal, published by AIPLA, http://www.aipla.org/Content/NavigationMenu/Publications/Quarterly_Journal1/Default800.htm

Science and Technology Law

ABA Section of Science and Technology Law, http://www.abanet.org/scitech/home.html
International Technology Law Association, http://www.itechlaw.org/
Cyberspace Bar Association, http://www.cyberbar.net/index.html
The National Academy of Science, Committee on Science, Technology, and Law, http://www.nationalacademies.org/
SciTech Lawyer, quarterly trade magazine published by the ABA Section, http://www.abanet.org/scitech/scitechlawyer.html

27

Entertainment Law

International Association of Entertainment Lawyers, http://www.iael.org/
Association of Media and Entertainment Counsel. http://www.theamec. com/
Black Entertainment and Sports Lawyers Association, http://www.besla. org/
ABA Forum Committee on the Entertainment and Sports Industries, http://www.abanet.org/forums/entsports/home.html
Entertainment and Sports Lawyer, published quarterly by the ABA Forum, http://www.abanet.org/forums/entsports/esl.html

Health Law

American Health Lawyers Association, http://www.healthlawyers.org/
ABA Health Law Section, http://www.abanet.org/health/home.html
Journal of Health and Life Sciences Law, quarterly trade journal published by AHLA, http://www.lexisnexis.com/ahla/ProductDetail. aspx?id=915
Health Lawyer, published by the ABA Health Law Section, http://www. abanet.org/health/03_publications/01_health_lawyer.html

Elder Law

National Academy of Elder Law Attorneys, http://www.naela.org
ABA Section of Real Property, Trust, and Estate Law; Elder Law, Disability Planning, and Bioethics Committee, http://www.abanet.org/dch/ committee.cfm?com=RP539000

Immigration Law

American Immigration Lawyers Association, http://www.aila.org
ABA Commission on Immigration, http://www.abanet.org/publicserv/ immigration/home.html
Immigration Law Today, bimonthly trade journal published by AILA, http:// www.aila.org/content/default.aspx?docid=8743

Labor and Employment Law

ABA Section of Labor and Employment Law, http://www.abanet.org/ labor/
Association of Corporate Counsel, Employment and Labor Law Committee, https://secure.acca.com/php/cms/index.php?id=100
National Employment Law Institute, http://www.neli.org/
Labor Lawyer, trade journal published by the ABA Section, http://www. bna.com/bnabooks/ababna/laborlawyer.htm

Administrative Law

ABA Section of Administrative Law and Regulatory Practice, http://www.abanet.org/adminlaw/home.html

Association of Administrative Law Judges, http://www.aalj.org/

National Association of Administrative Law Judiciary, http://www.naalj.org/

Administrative Law Review, published quarterly by the ABA Section, http://www.abanet.org/adminlaw/Adminlaw-review.html

CHAPTER 2

Nonprofit and Public Interest Careers

Plenty of anecdotal evidence suggests that many law students enter law school with the intention of entering a public service, legal aid, or nonprofit career upon graduation—yet few new graduates actually do. According to the National Association for Legal Career Professionals' employment patterns data, just 7.3 percent of women and 3.5 percent of men entered public service careers from the class of 2006. Still, that's an increase from previous classes: NALP (National Association for Law Placement) reports that in 1982, only 3.4 percent of women and 1.4 percent of men chose this line of work.

Somewhere along the way—perhaps due to vastly increasing law school tuitions and law student debt—those same students who seek to change the world on their law school admissions essays end up going for a higher paycheck in the private sector. According to "Lifting the Burden: Law Student Debt as a Barrier to Public Service," a report issued by the ABA Commission on Loan Repayment and Forgiveness, public service salaries have not kept pace with either private sector salaries or law student debt. The study reports that the median starting salary in private practice stood at ninety thousand dollars in 2002, while public service starting salaries stood at thirty-six thousand. As a result of rising tuition and debt, many new law grads simply can't enter public service or legal service careers.

And when it comes to needing capable and dedicated graduates, legal aid and public service agencies are desperate. "Many public service employers report having a difficult time attracting the best qualified law graduates," the ABA commission's report goes on to state. "Alternatively, those who do hire law graduates find that, because of educational debt payments, those whom they do hire leave just at the point when they provide the most valuable services."

And some studies suggest that some attorneys wish they could do more. "The inability to make a contribution to social good is the aspect of practice that seems to disappoint young lawyers the most," according to the ABA Young Lawyers Division Satisfaction Survey conducted in 2000. "A quarter of the responding young lawyers feel that their expectations with regard to their ability to make a contribution to social good through the practice of law have not been met, a situation which has not improved in the interval between surveys," the ABA survey goes on to say.

One solution to the problem lies in easing the debt burdens. The ABA Commission's report lists federal and state programs, law school scholarships and fellowships, after-graduation fellowships, and loan repayment assistance programs among the ways to help JDs enter a public service career and still pay their bills. However you work it out, if you choose public service, legal service, or nonprofit work, you are sure to find plenty of options.

Read on for others' experiences in this field.

Legal Aid Attorney

Jose Padilla is a man of his word. When he was applying to college at Stanford in 1970, Padilla asked a community religious leader for a letter of recommendation. The man said he would write the letter if Padilla promised to come back to his rural migrant community in California and bring his education back to the town for five years. Padilla made that promise and stayed true to it: After graduating from Stanford and UC Berkeley's Boalt Hall School of Law, he joined California Rural Legal Assistance (CRLA) and went back to work in Imperial County, serving the migrant worker community from which he came.

But he didn't just stay around for five years: Now executive director of CRLA, Padilla is still serving his community. "I knew that I was going to use law for the benefit of the community that raised me," he says. "I went to law school already with the idea that law could be used to bring about conditions of justice for communities that were important to me." CRLA represents people in labor and employment disputes, housing cases, family matters, and disability issues, among other things.

31

Padilla is just one of the many committed legal aid attorneys helping those who can't afford legal representation. Legal assistance programs offer JDs opportunities to work in a wide variety of fields and practice areas: representing victims of domestic violence, for example, or tenants in disputes over housing issues.

LEGAL AID ATTORNEY: SOME SUBSPECIALTIES

- Family law
- Domestic violence
- Housing law/landlord-tenant issues
- Rural law
- Immigration law
- Consumer protection
- Elder law
- Human rights
- Taxes
- Public benefits
- Health care access
- Juvenile law
- Economic development

For a comprehensive listing of legal aid providers in your state, see "Map of LSC Programs" on the Legal Services Corporation's website at http://www.lsc.gov/map/index.php

Padilla manages fifty-five attorneys at CRLA who are committed to bringing about social change for rural workers and their families. "What is exciting is when you create a space for these lawyers to bring about change in the lives of poor people [and] fight for something as esoteric as dignity and self-respect," he says. "On another level, we are trying to bring about systemic change for poor people."

Padilla recalls one case that led him to investigate sex discrimination among farm worker women. A woman walked in over a pay check dispute and brought it to Padilla's attention that many farm workers were forced to trade sex to get or keep their jobs; Padilla in turn brought the issue to the attention of the government and ended up getting verdicts in favor of women victims who sued. "All she wanted was two weeks' pay," he says, "but [she] got back what she had lost: her dignity as a woman."

LEGAL AID ATTORNEY: BREAK-IN TIP

Like many other lawyers in public service, Padilla is quick to dispel the myth that nonprofit or public interest lawyers are "second class." Rising law student debts, he says, make it increasingly hard to get started in legal aid after graduation; Padilla says that's a pity, as most students are at their most idealistic when they are fresh out of law school. "Know that you an contribute to public interest law in many different ways," he says, including pro bono work, financial contributions, or serving as co-counsel on large or complex cases where it isn't economically feasible for public interest lawyers to handle the entire case. "All these opportunities present themselves to a young lawyer," Padilla says.

In public interest law, attorneys have to be able to communicate and lawyer at many different levels: from talking with the client who isn't literate to "negotiating with lawyers that a high-powered corporation puts against you," says Padilla. "At the same time, you can put together policy," he says; for example, Padilla wrote California's education law for migrant children.

Padilla has a simple tip for young lawyers: "Write down what kind of lawyer you want to be," he says, "and [refer back to it] as you go about your career." He encourages those with an interest in legal aid to volunteer and find a connection with a client who needs their help the most—to remember the face of the poor client who was desperate for legal assistance. "You need that direct engagement at some point, because it turns the law into something different," Padilla says.

As a nonprofit lawyer, you also have the opportunity to benefit the arts: at "volunteer lawyers for the arts" organizations, attorneys represent artists, writers, and musicians, protecting the rights of arts and entertainment professionals in every discipline of the arts. "We make it our mission to ensure that our clients obtain the best representation available, regardless of ability to pay legal fees," explains Marci A. Rolnik, Legal Director of Lawyers for the Creative Arts in Chicago. "The issues are the same: each client needs competent counsel from attorneys who understand the nuances of the art and entertainment business. Our attorneys take an active interest in our clients' work, take it seriously, and as a result, are excellent advocates."

Being a nonprofit director, Rolnik's roles in the organization are multi-faceted, which she says is typical in nonprofit settings. "Most every non-profit organization is thinly staffed with a tremendous overlap of duties, and we are no exception," she explains. "We have a constant stream of both clients looking for assistance and lawyers willing to help, and I am the sieve in the middle: sorting out what cases take priority, digesting each presented legal issue, playing translator, researching issues, and providing support on both ends of the spectrum." Rolnik provides legal advice, drafts contracts, and mediates disputes. In addition, she works to "plan educational programs, assist with marketing and fundraising, and serve as a spokesman for pro bono investment in the arts. I also answer phones, make copies and labels, write correspondence, handle filing; it is very much like being a solo shop, except we all share in the overall mission."

Entertainment law is constantly changing, and Rolnik says she enjoys helping artists develop their talents. "The entertainment field is fascinating to me, simply because it is so dynamic," she says. "We don't know what to expect, and many of the old models no longer apply now that we have a constant proliferation of new media. The industry tries to track the dollars, primarily by following advertising budgets, but it is much more compelling to follow the artists and where ingenuity takes them to market and distribute their products."

As with any other nonprofit position, scarce resources and constantly having to find grants and funding keep Rolnik's job challenging. Still, Rolnik says she sees many attorneys eager to help out. "Every single day I am shocked and awed by the extraordinary dedication and generosity of the legal community," she says. "Every day I find lawyers or law students who want to do something to help. The public has some mistaken beliefs about greed in the legal field, but what I see every day is the exact opposite—law firms giving out millions of dollars of work product for free."

Rolnik says communication skills are essential for the job, adding that practical writing skills and the ability to "cut through language" have helped her the most. "I make it a business practice to always speak on my clients' level—to listen to them—and to read between the lines," Rolnik explains. "There are often more ways you can help than to give what someone is asking. I enjoy figuring out what could work and helping people to make connections to move projects forward." But above all, "[m]y biggest asset is my passion for what I do," says Rolnik. "I am excellent at motivating people to try and to do things both for themselves and for others."

BREAK-IN TIP:

Rolnik says that participating in a volunteer organization can lead to lucrative client referrals, particularly for lawyers who are just getting started in a field. "It has been said that I am 'every artist's best friend'—and every lawyer's, particularly those trying to break into the entertainment business," she notes. "I know for a fact that LCA client referrals have built a number of entertainment practices around town." To those just getting started, Rolnik recommends "You learn the most on any job by doing, and I would never expect that something I read would teach me the practicalities of real life application," she says. "New lawyers should be cautious and handle work within their comfort zones but also not be afraid by what they don't know. Be confident and know that there are more experienced lawyers out there to help you."

Rolnik emphasizes that nonprofit work means long hours and lots of work, but adds that the job's rewards make it all worth it. "I am stressed out almost every day, and I can't return every call. That gets to me. But what I give of myself to my clients is without value. They always say thank you," she says. "I love being the person to make that possible, and I try to remind myself that my energy, time, and effort really make a difference. Through LCA, I have been able to significantly affect the lives of thousands of artists with nowhere else to turn."

Public Defender

John Stuart's career revelation came in front of a juvenile detention center. Then a teacher at an inner-city high school in Philadelphia, Stuart was walking past the center and was stopped by a group of his students who had been arrested and placed in detention. "John, get us out of here," the kids pleaded. That was enough to send the teacher to law school in upstate New York, and he got there just in time for a call for volunteers in the famed Attica Brothers case. Stuart landed a position as a law clerk, working with one of his professors who served as the head of the Attica Brothers' legal defense team. "It guided my system that I was going to be a public defender," Stuart says.

After graduating law school, Stuart worked as a trial court public defender in Minnesota, and in 1990, he was appointed as the state public defender, head of the public defense services for the entire state. Working

35

in that position ever since, Stuart says most of his work deals with supervising the attorneys who make up the state's ten judicial district public defense operations. All in all, Stuart oversees about 175,000 cases per year. He also advocates for public defense at the legislature, performs training, and oversees strategic planning.

One benefit to being a public defender is the learning experience: Indigent clients need legal help on a vast variety of matters. As a public defender, Stuart tried every case under the sun, from underage drinking to first degree murder. He says it took him a while to find his voice in the courtroom, and he still misses representing clients and the immediacy of client contact he experienced as a public defender. In fact, he hopes to get back to his initial calling when he retires: working as a juvenile court defender.

Avis E. Buchanan's first taste of public defender work also came in law school: The Harvard Law student was recruited by Charles Ogletree to work at the newly created Public Defender Service (PDS) in Washington, D.C., for a summer. After serving in a judicial clerkship for a year after graduation, Buchanan spent six and a half years in PDS's trial division, working on everything from juvenile matters to felony cases. Today, she is PDS's director, and most of her work is administrative: supervision, drafting policy, finances and budget oversight, working with PDS's board of directors, and representing the organization in the criminal justice community.

One of the greatest challenges Stuart faces comes from what he calls the "demonization of his clientele." "We've moved from a person who's in jail being an ordinary person who made a mistake to the idea that the person who's charged or convicted of a crime is like a monster who's from another planet," Stuart explains. He says that has made it difficult to pass constructive criminal justice legislation and represent his clients' interests.

But as most public defenders can assert, the field presents plenty of opportunities for bettering the criminal justice system—and one's own career in the process. "I like working with people who are trying to create something better, whether it's in the direct representation of people or in criminal justice policy," says Stuart. Buchanan agrees. "Working with clients in and of itself is rewarding," she says, "and knowing that you are making a difference in clients' lives [is even more so]."

Stuart recalls one juvenile defendant, a young Native American woman who had been adopted by a white family. Experiencing problems related to identity in high school, the woman was arrested several times and finally sent to a girls reform school. When she was arrested again for breaking out of the school and stealing a car, Stuart represented her on a motion to keep her from being transferred to adult court: He says she had been caught in the basement of her birth county's courthouse, poring over birth certificate records. Stuart developed a plan that convinced the judge to keep the young woman in juvenile court. Years later, Stuart ran into the woman on the street: She was working, married, and a new mother—a success story that touched Stuart's heart.

But Stuart notes that not every story ends so well. "You also get a lot of loss and disappointment in this work," he says. "It helps to be an optimist; it helps to believe that every person has some good in them."

PUBLIC DEFENDER: DIFFERENT TYPES OF SYSTEMS (AND EMPLOYERS)

Buchanan says there are many different approaches to public defense work across the country. While some states hire private attorneys to take on indigent clients on a contract basis, others employ a public defender system that houses full-time attorneys.

"One of the most important functions I have is hiring the attorneys here," Buchanan says. "Our reputation rides on them [and] the continuity of the talent pool has to be upheld." Buchanan says she looks for candidates who are great writers, have excellent problem-solving skills, and are creative and passionate about what they want to do. Recognizing and solving issues are also important to her, as are the ability to relate to clients, cooperate, and work in a team environment. She also says that she uses language skills, like Spanish and sign language, on the job.

PUBLIC DEFENDER: BREAK-IN TIP

"Try to expose yourself to the field directly so that you have a truer understanding of [what is involved]," Buchanan counsels. She recommends starting as a law clerk and believes her own summer clerkship at PDS made a difference in getting hired after graduation. "It's a job where you can use every bit of your life experience," says Stuart. "The most interesting people we get are people who've had a previous career dealing with a diverse group of folks."

There's no question that indigent defense is a rewarding career, as are public interest careers in general. "You're using your legal

37

skills for clients who really, really need a good lawyer," says Stuart. "You're thinking on your feet. . . . It's a job that will keep you energized for decades." For many public interest lawyers, the greatest reward is knowing that their work has an impact. "It's important; it's valuable," says Buchanan about public defense. "It makes a valuable contribution."

Nonprofit Director

JDs don't just serve the greater good as nonprofit lawyers; they also help by serving as directors or leaders at nonprofit organizations.

For Diane Chin, being a nonprofit director "was a good skill match," she says. "I really like thinking about organizational systems and how to create processes within an organization . . . that allow work to go forward but also create a [positive] environment for your attorneys." As director of Equal Justice Works/West in San Francisco, Chin does just that: She helps create models for new lawyers who want to pursue public interest careers and assists them with the training they need. After working in private practice for ten years, Chin started out in nonprofit management at a civil rights advocacy group; she then helped found the Public Interest Law Center at Stanford Law School; she also coauthored the book *Beyond the Big Firm: Profiles of Lawyers Who Want More* (Aspen, 2007).

Chin says all of her previous experiences in public interest law allow her not only to provide substantive knowledge in her current position but also to possess an understanding of public interest law careers—which in turn helps her better counsel other lawyers who are interested in nonprofit work. Chin says communication skills are essential in her role as director of a nonprofit because she needs to be able to reach a wide audience, from lawyers to people in the community.

"Nonprofit management can be difficult just because you're balancing so many interests," Chin says. "Also, getting sufficient resources is always a challenge." But she says helping her organization grow and developing programs for lawyers is rewarding. "I entered the field hoping that I could bring some skills, some passion, and some compassion in terms of helping clients . . . and assisting people to achieve their goals," she says.

Chin says some of her most fulfilling work came from representing victims of hate crimes, such as people who were threatened in their own

---

NONPROFIT MANAGEMENT: BREAK-IN TIP

To get involved in nonprofit management, Chin says that a candidate must "learn to be an effective manager." She recommends getting started by managing small organizations, serving on boards or bar associations, or even getting involved in the local school system or other community organization—the important thing is learning to manage and run things. "Be creative in terms of learning how to manage people and to delegate," she says. "Learn about yourself as a manager and what that requires." There isn't a single path that gets people involved in nonprofit work, Chin adds; she says some get started in fellowships, through clinical experience in law school, or pro bono programs.

---

neighborhoods. "There's something extraordinarily satisfying about representing a client who has previously dreaded going home," she says. Like most other lawyers working in nonprofit organizations, Chin finds her field rife with rewarding opportunities.

Nonprofit Pioneers

Some JDs carve out unique niches for themselves within the nonprofit or public interest field.

Take John P. Fischer, for example. As founder and executive director of the National Employment Law Institute (NELI) in Denver, Colorado, he offers seminars and continuing legal education programs for attorneys nationwide. Fischer started NELI in 1976, after working extensively in nonprofit organizations, including running an affirmative action clearinghouse and an annual seminar on EEOC issues. Though at first he hung out his shingle as well—thinking NELI would be fun to run for just a few years—Fischer says he was offering programs nationwide just three years after getting started and has been doing so ever since.

"We've carved out a niche that no one else has gotten into," says Fischer. "Over the last thirty years, there has not been a more dynamic area of the law than employment law." As NELI's executive director, Fischer puts together programs, conducts seminars, helps line up speakers and instructors, and follows up on presentations after they are given. "There's nothing more rewarding than putting together a seminar and having people fill out an evaluation and tell you that this is the best seminar they've been to throughout their careers," he says.

39

"I knew while I was in law school that I wanted to be both a teacher and a lawyer who helps people," says Lawrence (Lonny) Rose, president and CEO of the National Institute for Trial Advocacy (NITA) in Louisville, Colorado, which provides training programs and publications to lawyers nationwide. "Even though I went into private practice, I began to teach almost immediately and began to volunteer at nonprofit organizations." Rose soon became a full-time professor, then went on to work in legal aid. In 1975, he was a participant in one of NITA's programs and recognized that NITA was the kind of organization he wanted to volunteer for; he eventually went in as a full-time administrator and later became the organization's president.

"To me, the practice of law and public service are just bound up together in one package," Rose says. As NITA's president, he oversees fund-raising and the delivery of programs and publications, and he ensures "that the educational and service mission of the organization is followed," he says. "The most rewarding part of my job is giving young lawyers the opportunity to learn and give back to their communities."

NONPROFIT INSTITUTIONS: BREAK-IN TIP

"If you're going into an existing organization, you have to know the history of the organization, how they got to where they are, and how they're carrying out their primary [goals]," says Fischer. He warns against going into a nonprofit that may be carried out improperly and says law grads interested in a nonprofit should check out their potential employers. If you're interested in starting your own nonprofit, be sure you investigate whether there is truly a need for something new in the area you want to offer: Does it already exist, and if so, would it make more sense for you to join an existing organization instead? "If you're going to pick a niche, make sure it's one that's needed, where there isn't already an organization that [serves those needs]," says Fischer. Also check out available resources about the various tasks that are involved in founding a nonprofit, such as gaining nonprofit status, grant-writing, fund-raising, and nonprofit management.

For Fischer, the hardest part of starting a nonprofit organization was building a reputation. "Even though there was a need for the service, people who are coming to the programs are spending real money and their time," he says, adding that he didn't pay himself a salary for the first three years. Rose cites fund-raising as his greatest challenge on the job. "There are lots of organizations that we compete with for the fund-raising money, and providing training for lawyers is not high on the list of giving money," he explains. But "if you help one lawyer, that one lawyer might help [many] people," he says.

Rose recommends that students and lawyers interested in nonprofit work figure out a niche or a community they'd like to serve and then volunteer their time generously to gain experience in the field. Those interested in nonprofit work must "be empathetic and recognize that others come before themselves," Rose says. They must be "willing to commit the time and effort to work on behalf of people who don't have a voice."

Legislator

Lawyers don't just analyze and apply the law—in many cases, they also write it.

Raised in a family that valued public service and with a legislator father, Mike Bishop had always thought that he would one day serve in office as well. Bishop practiced criminal law after graduating law school in 1992, then slowly went into real estate law and finally a business law practice. In 1998, Bishop was elected to the Michigan State House of Representatives and served two terms; now, he's on his second term in the Michigan State Senate and serves as senate majority leader. "One of the things that got me into the practice of law was helping people and solving problems," Bishop explains. "I do that now on a much larger scale."

Helping constituents is also the most fulfilling part of Morgan Carroll's job as a legislator in the Colorado State House of Representatives. Carroll started out practicing civil and consumer litigation, partnered with her mother in their own firm. Carroll says clients would ask her about an issue they found unfair, and while she wanted to help, she would hit a wall and have no place to refer the clients but the legislature. So Carroll decided to take matters into her own hands—in 2004 (just four years after graduating law school), she was elected to the legislature. Carroll now serves sixty-six thousand constituents. She holds two town hall meetings per month, reads approximately eight hundred bills per year while the legislature is in session, and typically authors about five bills per session.

In addition to their legislative duties, both Bishop and Carroll maintain their private law practices. In fact, Bishop says his bills sometimes have a direct connection to his clients. For example, he authored Michigan's identity theft protection bill after representing clients who had fallen victim to identity theft. While the legislature is in session, Carroll

41

meets with clients on the weekends and handles cases in the evenings. "One [challenge] is time management, especially if you need another job," she says.

In legislative work, "sometimes there aren't any clear answers," says Bishop. "It's different from practicing law." Bishop recalls being a prosecutor and having to prove each element of an offense before the jury could come back with a guilty verdict. "In my practice in the law, you had to prove yourself and come through on your promises before the jury voted for you," he says. As a legislator you get the people's vote of confidence before doing the job.

Another challenge in legislative work is balancing the interests of the people with "institutional things that make reform for the 'little guys' tougher than it has to be," says Carroll; she cites dealing with paid lobbyists' advocacy power as an example of a frustration. Carroll says it has taken her five years to get protection for whistle-blowers in the health care field protection, and three years to give people the right to choose a doctor if they get hurt on the job—still, she says the end result of helping people makes the work worthwhile.

LEGISLATOR: BREAK-IN TIP

If you're interested in becoming a legislator, "know your district," says Carroll, "know the numbers . . . the term limits, and who is term limited when." Also, get involved, Bishop and Carroll both recommend: Attend meetings, sit on committees, and be visible as someone who helps the community. "You need to be a good listener," Carroll adds. "You need to be a critical thinker and be willing to ask critical questions," which she says is more important than knowing all the answers.

The JD degree is helpful in legislative work. "I have a better handle on negotiating," says Bishop. "I deal with the opposition better because of my training and education." Bishop says that many people assume the legislature is made up entirely of lawyers, which isn't the case: He says his session only has a handful of JDs. "Lawyers often do well as legislators," says Carroll; she adds that a legal education makes it easier to read proposed legislation or materials from lobbyists and understand any inconsistencies or shortcomings.

"The most important advice you could have is not to hold yourself back," says Carroll. "You don't have to go in knowing everything.

You can get help with campaigns; you can get help with the legislative process."

Career Options at Legal Trade Associations

What's the recipe for a successful career as a legal association attorney? You need to know and understand your particular field and be able to represent the interests of your association's members.

Susan Hackett practiced at a law firm after graduation, and while she loved the firm, she didn't love practicing. "I started to think a lot about how I would find something that would allow me to use my legal education but not in the [law firm] environment," she says. Hackett saw a notice on a law school job board looking for an entry-level attorney to handle publications and programs for the American Corporate Counsel Association (now Association of Corporate Counsel, or ACC). Hackett was intrigued and went for an interview; she says she was excited to help brainstorm and develop new resources for the in-house community.

"There wasn't a job description except to create stuff," Hackett recounts. "That's what I've always loved about this place . . . we continue to create stuff." Hackett says she has helped develop ACC's community resources across the board. "I've done everything from CLE development to substantive resource development, to developing the website," she says. Hackett has also handled advocacy work, programming, and serving as "the voice of the in-house bar." Over time, Hackett started handling the growing association's legal needs, which eventually evolved into her current role as general counsel.

Fred Krebs's entire legal career has centered on nonprofit organizations—he's served them as in-house counsel, lobbyist, policy and research associate, and outside counsel serving nonprofit clients. As president of ACC, Krebs now oversees the organization's management, including communications, human resources, membership development, fund-raising, and corporate governance. He also serves as an "evangelist" for the organization, he says, and works with the board of directors "trying to [chart] the road ahead, and where we want to be."

Hackett says it's not unusual for lawyers at trade and nonprofit associations to take on many other roles in addition to counseling—so those interested in this field might be well served by staying broad and learning to be a jack-of-all-trades, she says. "It's one of the last places where you truly get to be the general counsel and chief cook and bottle washer at the same time," says Hackett. "You're looking for ways to move the bar forward." Hackett says her job description can change as the needs

43

and interests of the in-house bar evolve—so what she does today may not be what she'll be doing in a year.

CAREERS AT LEGAL TRADE ASSOCIATIONS: SOME SUBSPECIALTIES

- Spokesperson
- Corporate counsel
- Writer or editor
- Manager
- Lobbyist
- Marketer
- Sales
- Human resources

Hackett says one of her greatest challenges on the job is staying grounded and "making sure you don't get out too far in front. It's finding that right mix of helping [members] when it's applicable . . . but also making sure that you're not the only one leading and no one's following."

For Hackett, the most fulfilling part of the job is working with the people she represents and experiencing "the level of talent and compassion, intellect and judgment that I see in the in-house bar," she says. "I get to work with interesting people; I get to work on interesting issues; and I get to travel to interesting places," Krebs adds. "I'm in an organization where my law degree is important because it's an organization for lawyers," which Krebs says was one of the things that attracted him to the position.

CAREERS AT LEGAL ASSOCIATIONS: BREAK-IN TIP

Many people get started in a trade association after working in the particular field that the association represents—for example, someone working at a technology law association may come from a technology law background. "It's important to be somewhere where you like the substance of what the organization does," says Krebs, and have "some buy-in to the philosophy and goals of the organization." Geography also has a lot to do with getting started, Hackett and Krebs both say. Trade associations tend to be clustered in a handful of cities, including Washington, D.C., and Chicago.

Krebs believes his past experiences helped him land the job at ACC. "I was very fortunate in my first position as associate general counsel at the U.S. Chamber of Commerce [to be] exposed to a wide range of opportunities," he explains, including lobbying, legislative efforts, and in-house lawyering. Krebs advises new law grads and those thinking of a career change to view each job as a stepping-stone and learning opportunity—even if the job isn't what they want to do for the rest of their careers. Think about "what it is that I'm going to learn and be exposed to here that will take me to the next step in my career," he says.

THERE'S MORE ON THE WEB!
Career Resources for This Chapter

National Legal Aid and Defender Association, http://www.nlada.org/

Equal Justice Works, http://www.equaljusticeworks.org/

Legal Services Corporation, http://www.lsc.gov/

ABA Division for Legal Services, http://www.abanet.org/legalservices/home.html

ABA Standing Committee on Pro Bono and Public Service, http://www.abanet.org/legalservices/probono/home.html

National Association of Pro Bono Professionals, http://www.abanet.org/legalservices/probono/napbpro/home.html

Dialogue Magazine, published by the ABA Division for Legal Services, http://www.abanet.org/legalservices/dialogue/

PSLawNet, NALP's Public Service Law Network, http://www.pslawnet.org/

ABA Division for Bar Services, http://www.abanet.org/barserv/

Bar Leader, news magazine published by the ABA Division for Bar Services, http://www.abanet.org/barserv/barleader.html

CHAPTER 3

Growing Government Careers

The money may be less, but for many attorneys working in public sector or government careers, the rewards are plenty: That's the general message in the *2007–2008 Federal Legal Employment Opportunities Guide*, published by NALP, the ABA Section of Government and Public Sector Lawyers, and the Partnership for Public Service. That guide estimates that through 2009, over ninety-six hundred new legal jobs will be created in eighteen agencies in the federal government alone, including such agencies as the Department of Justice, Department of Treasury, and the Department of Homeland Security.

Despite the growth in government openings for JDs, NALP reports a slight decline in the percentage of law graduates entering government jobs. While 12.8 percent of male grads in 1982 entered government, only 11.7 percent did so in 2006; among women, the numbers in 1982 stood at 14.2 percent, but only 12.2 percent in 2006. The decline among minority grads is even greater, going from 21 percent in 1982 to 12.6 percent in 2006.

One benefit that might entice public service–minded individuals is a federal loan repayment assistance program. According to the *2007– 2008 Federal Legal Employment Opportunities Guide*, federal employees can receive up to ten thousand dollars per year—sixty thousand dollars total— in loan repayment assistance, in return for committing to three years of service. In addition, government jobs tend to offer great experience, better quality of life, and often a "foot in the door" for able law grads, the guide reports.

But federal jobs aren't the only government options for skilled JDs. Career opportunities also exist in state and local government law, including prosecution, municipal law, and state and local administrative law. Military judge advocate generals' corps also hire attorneys.

Below is just a sampling of some of the many career opportunities available to JDs in public service and government work.

Homeland Security Careers

Increased attention paid to national security means growing job opportunities for attorneys in the field. Homeland security attorneys and advisors work in a variety of subspecialties, including administrative immigration law and immigration law enforcement, public contracts and procurement, and customs and border protection.

Joe Whitley began his government career as a state prosecutor, then became a U.S. attorney in the early 1980s, prosecuting federal cases. From there, he went on to work for the Department of Justice as an attorney, then went back to federal prosecution in Atlanta. In 2002, Whitley was tapped to become general counsel of the newly created Department of Homeland Security.

"The office I supervised has approximately seventeen hundred lawyers," says Whitley. Some, he says, work for the Federal Emergency Management Agency, assisting with disaster declaration and getting funds to affected areas. Others work for the Coast Guard's judge advocate general's office, often dealing with military and admiralty law issues as well as national security questions. Homeland security attorneys may also specialize in immigration law: providing legal advice to the Citizenship and Immigration Services Office; handling removal (formerly deportation) hearings; or working with the Immigrations and Customs Enforcement Office. Still others work in customs and border protection, dealing with duties, the movement of goods and people across borders, or searches and seizures and constitutional rights at the border.

Depending on their subspecialties, homeland security attorneys must possess a distinct set of skills. For example, Whitley says immigration enforcement specialists who often handle a heavy case load in immigration court must be experts in evidence law, while procurement or public

47

contracts attorneys must know contract law. Most attorneys who work for the Department of Homeland Security come into their positions with some legal experience, says Whitley; he adds that people with experience usually get seniority over entry-level attorneys, and that experience may translate even if it isn't exactly on point—for instance, regulatory or administrative experience at another agency.

HOMELAND SECURITY CAREERS: SOME SUBSPECIALTIES

- Customs and border protection
- Emergency management
- Public contracts and procurement
- Military law
- Admiralty law
- Administrative immigration law
- Immigration law enforcement
- Constitutional rights dealing with national security

Whitley says those interested in homeland security must be able to collaborate with others well. "A sharpness and the ability to render a decision as promptly as possible is critical, too," he says, explaining that the field requires quick thinking and rapid decision-making at times. In most positions, some level of government or security clearance will be required. "The background check depends on the position and the degree to which the person might be dealing with classified information," Whitley says.

HOMELAND SECURITY CAREERS: BREAK-IN TIP

Federal agencies are not the only place to begin a career in homeland security. Whitley says that every state has a homeland security director, and most of them have positions for attorneys that are comparable to the ones available federally. Some municipalities might also have similar positions. "Get some exposure someplace," Whitley recommends; that will help you get a position more easily on the federal side.

There are plenty of challenges in homeland security, Whitley says. Some people, for example, see homeland security lawyers—and government lawyers in general, says Whitley—as partisan. During his tenure, Whitley says he made it his goal to make the department more client-friendly and proactive, and to hire lawyers who are knowledgeable about their clients' needs, based on merit and confidence. He recalls helping the Coast Guard implement new maritime regulations in one instance, and says he was pleased by all of the positive feedback he received.

To Whitley, a homeland security career is one of the greatest ways to make a lasting and significant contribution to the safety of his country. "The underpinning of [a safer nation] is the legal system," he says. "Homeland security is at the epicenter of making sure that will be in place for the [future]."

Prosecutor

Though she's just four years out of law school, Lindsey Koches is already making strides in government work. A senior deputy attorney at the Bucks County District Attorney's Office in Pennsylvania, Koches serves as chief of the adult sex crimes unit and focuses primarily on sexual offenses and child abuse cases.

Most prosecutors start out with basic cases, but Koches found she quickly moved away from common crimes and began to specialize. "You learn very quickly," Koches says, adding she had just about a half hour to prepare for her first trial—a felony drug case. "It was tough. It really is sink or swim, but it's just so much more rewarding," she says. "You can make all the money in the world, but if you don't like what you're doing, it's not going to be worth it." Koches enjoys feeling like she is making the community safer through her work. She also finds it rewarding to be able to work on such a wide variety of cases and get direct trial experience every day.

Representing the state's interests, Koches prosecutes cases from investigation to the post-trial period, and is in court on most days. She brings and responds to pretrial motions, prepares victims and witnesses for trial, and conducts voir dire. Much of her day is also spent collecting and poring over evidence—she remembers one recent trial where she handled 86 pieces of evidence on numerous pretrial issues. In addition to the seventy-hour workweek she often puts in at the office, Koches can also be on call at night or over the weekend.

PROSECUTION: SOME EMPLOYERS

- State attorney generals' offices
- County district attorneys' offices
- United States attorneys' offices
- Local or municipal attorneys' offices

The most frustrating part of Koches's job is when she works hard to get a conviction but still loses. "In law school, when you do your work, you tend to do well," she says. "It's not always so in real life." She recalls her first big loss, a rape case against a married airline pilot who was accused of having sex with a fifteen-year-old girl. "People don't realize how far [you have to go] to get a conviction," says Koches. She says juries often expect "CSI treatment": They want to see DNA evidence and the like, or else they won't convict, no matter how well the state presents its case.

PROSECUTION: BREAK-IN TIP

To get started in prosecution, Koches recommends trial experience; courses like Evidence and Case Preparation can be valuable. Candidates should be comfortable in the courtroom, she says—the more confident you are, the more faith a jury will have in you. Plus, they have to be persuasive yet tactful, especially when explaining to victims why they will take certain courses of action. It's best to get an internship in your local district attorney's office before considering a full-time position, Koches says.

A career as a prosecutor can not only get you started in government but also provide valuable courtroom experience, which can translate into job openings in the public or private sectors. But Koches warns that the job can be difficult and exhausting. "It's a rewarding job and a lot of fun, but it isn't for everyone," she says.

Regulatory Careers in Government

With her undergraduate background in chemistry, Linda Lasley thought she would turn into an intellectual property lawyer upon graduating from law school in 1995. Instead, she developed an interest in environmental law as a law student, and practiced as a state government environmental enforcement and regulatory attorney. She transferred to the attorney general's office, where she pursued civil actions in environmental law; later, she also served as an environmental law judge.

REGULATORY CAREERS IN GOVERNMENT: SOME SUBSPECIALTIES

The ABA Section of Administrative Law and Regulatory Practice lists the following government functions committees:

- Agriculture
- Antitrust and Trade Regulation
- Banking and Financial Services
- Benefits
- Beverage Alcohol Practice
- Communications
- Consumer Products Regulation
- Criminal Process
- Education
- Elections
- Energy
- Environmental and Natural Resources Regulation
- Food and Drug
- Government Personnel
- Health and Human Service
- Homeland Security and National Defense
- Housing and Urban Development
- Immigration and Naturalization
- Insurance
- Intellectual Property
- International Law
- International Trade and Customs
- Labor and Employment Law
- Ombuds
- Postal Matters
- Securities, Commodities, and Exchanges
- Transportation
- Treasury, Revenue, and Tax
- Veterans Affairs

With all of that government work behind her, it's no surprise that Lasley landed a regulatory position with the federal government: She now serves as assistant chief counsel, Legislation and Regulations Division at the U.S. Department of Transportation, after spending five years working for the department's general counsel. She says she was transferred to the Federal Transit Administration to help ramp up the agency's regulatory practice.

"I grew up in a family where public service was important," Lasley explains. "Through law school, I realized that private practice wasn't going to be my strength." Lasley says she enjoys serving the public interest and finds great diversity in her work in administrative law and regulatory practice.

In her current position, Lasley oversees four attorneys, legal staff, and student interns. Taking her direction from Congress most of the time, Lasley answers attorneys' and others' questions about administrative procedure; helps write and implement new regulations; briefs regional counsel on new regulations and the advice they should give about those regulations; and keeps the agency's chief counsel informed of issues and new decisions. Also check out the section on administrative law careers in Chapter 1.

"One misconception [about government work] is that you work nine to five, with no overtime, and [that] it's all about pushing paper," says Lasley. She says she expects great customer service from herself and those working for her, and feels it's important to work toward "trying to debunk the whole bureaucracy myth."

REGULATORY CAREERS IN GOVERNMENT: BREAK-IN TIP

"Do your research because there are so many programs the government sponsors that will get your foot in the door," Lasley says. She cites her department's Honors Attorney Program as an example; she also says that internships and volunteer positions can be a good way to get started. Course work in administrative law—whether in law school or through CLE—can also help. "A lot of students avoid administrative law and think it's not going to impact them," Lasley says. "It's not just this little, narrow slice. It impacts so many areas."

Once you're hired, Lasley stresses the importance of being willing to perform whatever task is needed. "I pitch in any way I can to get the job done," she says. She also says that folks, even student interns, who take on challenging projects and perform well are more likely to be promoted and rise up in the ranks.

But mastering one subspecialty in administrative law doesn't necessarily mean you'll be confined to that area for life—administrative skills can translate well into work at other government agencies, and even private practice. Lasley's story illustrates one's ability to take administrative skills from one agency to another: She transferred her experience in environmental law into a successful career in transportation law. "Once you learn [administrative law], this is something you can take to any agency," she says. "You can really make a career out of it."

Careers in State and Local Government Law

Federal and state governments aren't the only places in government where JDs are needed. Many local and municipal governments also hire JDs for various positions: city attorneys and solicitors, auditors, and city prosecutors, just to name a few. Typically, municipal attorneys are elected, though some are appointed; towns and cities may also have requirements for the position in place.

Garry Hunter started as a municipal lawyer around the time he hung out his shingle after moving to a new community. He was elected as Athens City law director in 1977 in Athens City, Ohio, and served in the position for thirty years. Because the city attorney position was part-time, Hunter says he could develop his private practice and serve his community at the same time. For example, with the help of his business degree, he became counsel to a small credit union in Ohio and slowly built up his practice. Today, Hunter says that credit union is a $200 million business and one of the city's major financial players.

In his position as city law director, Hunter attended daily meetings, answered emails, and tended to all of the city's legal needs in-house. In addition to serving as legal counsel to all of the city's departments, including the auditor, mayor, and treasurer, Hunter served as supervisor of the city prosecutors and legal counsel to the city's school district.

But you don't even have to work for the government to have a successful career in state or local government law. Benjamin Griffiths is a partner at Griffiths & Griffiths in Cleveland, Missouri. Though he is in private practice, Griffiths also serves as board attorney for a joint water

53

management district and says that his work covers everything from state and federal civil litigation to administrative and regulatory practice.

"'Typical' does not describe what I do in my current positions," explains Griffiths. "I am the senior partner in a firm of four attorneys, with a state and local government practice focusing on representation of governmental entities and officials, insureds and insurers in the areas of election law, voting rights, civil rights, public sector insurance coverage and insurance defense, premises security liability claims, construction defect claims, and environmental law."

Griffiths began his municipal law career right out of law school, representing state and local government clients—including municipalities, special districts, and government boards—in a variety of civil cases. After his firm merged with another in 1977, a partner at the firm invited Griffiths to serve as his assistant in representing the county board of supervisors, the county's governing authority. When that partner left, Griffiths took over as the board's attorney and hasn't looked back since. In fact, during his first year on the job, Griffiths led one of the country's first voting dilution cases under the amended Voting Rights Act. Following that trial, "I served as lead counsel in a dozen or more voting rights cases on behalf of school districts and counties, then was asked to represent other local governments in Mississippi, Maryland, Florida, Texas, South Carolina, and other jurisdictions over the next two decades," Griffiths says. "The most gratifying part of this work in the field of voting rights and election law was the diversity and broad scope of federal civil litigation that brought me into regular and sustained contact with the Civil Rights Division of the U.S. Department of Justice and exposed me to some of the best voting rights attorneys and experts in the nation."

MUNICIPAL OR LOCAL ATTORNEY: SOME SUBSPECIALTIES

The ABA Section of State and Local Government Law lists the following committees:

- Condemnation
- Environmental Law
- Government Operations
- Homeland Security
- Land Use Planning and Zoning
- Public Education
- Public Finance

As a municipal attorney, Hunter says he was thrown into a job that often required him to be a jack-of-all-trades. "My first case was a three-mile jurisdictional fight with the County of Athens," he says. "Before I was elected, the longtime Athens County prosecutor had issued an opinion that the City of Athens did not have planning jurisdiction in the three-mile area outside of Athens City." His predecessor decided not to fight the court case and agreed to a summary judgment, but Hunter took the county on and won. He also gained experience in employment negotiations, tax abatements, and local government law. And because his position oversaw the city's school district, Hunter says he also gained valuable insight into school law in general and education law for the handicapped.

Griffiths describes the field of municipal law as one that is challenging yet rewarding. "It is dynamic, presents constant challenges, and enables me to focus my law practice on those areas of the law in which I believe I can effectively serve the public and the bar," he notes, "and perhaps do my part to improve the civil justice system and promote transparent democratic government both domestically and internationally."

Hunter also says he's seen many rewards in his municipal law career. "This was probably the luckiest move of my life," he states. "The variety of work is great, [and] the opportunity to improve your fellow citizens' quality of life and to make a meaningful difference in your community is very rewarding." He says the position afforded him free publicity in local media, free training in government law by experts, and great stature as an attorney because he represented two of the largest employers in his county: the City of Athens and the city's school district.

As in any public office, municipal attorneys face some challenges. "The greatest challenge I face in these fields of law is to keep current, maintaining a level of proficiency, competence, and knowledge in my area of expertise," Griffiths says. "Even though I have been able to narrow my field of practice to a handful of specific areas of the law, the massive amount of change that I see on a daily basis is staggering." To keep current, Griffiths says he reads and writes for various legal periodicals; attends continuing education and networking events and sometimes serves as a speaker; keeps in close contact with his senators and representative; and maintains a relationship with several law schools and trade organizations. "All of these provide the sources and means of maintaining a fairly comprehensive understanding of the many components and potential developments that affect my law practice," lists Griffiths.

"The time pressures are great, and the life of a public official means you are always on public display and subject to public criticism," Hunter explains. "This can be difficult for those who are faint of heart, and certainly can be difficult for your family, [especially] children." Griffiths says he also faces time pressures, particularly when it comes to holding down a full-time law practice while serving on the board of various professional organizations—he serves as chair of the ABA Section of State and Local Government Law, among other obligations. "There are twenty-four hours in each day, and I sometimes feel that I need forty-eight," he confesses.

Griffiths stresses the importance of networking, reaching out to other attorneys, and joining professional groups. "In law school, I learned how to find the law; I certainly did not learn all that I needed to know in order to develop a successful and meaningful practice," he notes. "The juris doctor degree opened doors for me, much as a key unlocks a door—but the work that I had to do and the practical knowledge, background and 'context' that I gained over these past thirty-three years, professionally, in my community, and through my many associations with lawyers, judges, and others, provided the means through which I gained the experience and ability to do what I do now."

MUNICIPAL OR LOCAL ATTORNEY: BREAK-IN TIP

"Starting in local government law is done in one of three ways," Hunter believes: "Take a job with a large metropolitan law firm and specialize in one particular aspect of local government law such as municipal bonding; take a job with the attorney general's office, state auditor's office, or a state government agency and specialize [in] one particular aspect of the local government law; or take a prosecutor's job in a municipality and work your way into the civil division and be a jack-of-all-trades in local government law."

People skills and communication skills are essential for the job, Hunter says, and candidates must be able to deal with the media and with being in the public eye, as well as to multitask and handle pressure well. Griffiths also stresses the importance of fine-tuning one's communication skills and shares two ways that have helped him. "First, jury trials require a defense attorney to listen, learn, perceive, and react to the dynamics of a six-member (federal court) or twelve-member (state court) group of people drawn at random from a jury pool that is supposed to reflect a cross section of a community," he states. "Second, representing boards, agencies, and commissions of elected and appointed officials requires an attorney to balance and assess competing interests while devoting energy, attention, and intellectual discernment to the problems, needs, and concerns of many people with many agendas. These two avenues have provided me with over three decades of career development and fine-tuning of communication skills."

For those interested in state or local government law, Griffiths says getting involved in professional organizations is essential. "Affiliate with a peer-review organization that provides opportunities to write newsworthy legal articles or comments, as well as opportunities to come into regular contact with lawyers whose practices relate to state and local government law," he recommends. Some attorneys, Griffiths notes, get started in the field by working as an aide or staffer for an elected official.

Internships can be another good way to break into municipal law. "I would suggest doing an internship in a public office or just volunteering for a public position like being on a recreation board, zoning board, planning commission, or some other volunteer public position," advises Hunter. "You can also easily get hired to work in a city prosecutor's office. Even if this is not what you want to do, it opens the door to a public sector career."

Military Attorney

It's often said that young lawyers want to change the world, and for some, that opportunity presents itself in a palpable way. Take navy lieutenant commander Susan McGarvey, for example: While in Iraq in December 2006, she had the chance to advise the Regime Crime Liaison Office on human rights standards dealing with Saddam Hussein's proposed execution. "To be involved in that on such a level," she says, "it took a few days to sink in."

McGarvey was commissioned by the navy during the fall of 1998, shortly after graduating law school—that's actually later than most, she says, as many people know whether they've been hired even before graduation. McGarvey first attended the navy's Officer Indoctrination Program (now its Officer Development School), where she learned about becoming a military officer, from wearing a uniform properly to understanding basic military structure. As if law school wasn't enough of a boot camp, she also learned to march, salute, get in formation, and perform physical tasks like sit-ups, push-ups, and running one and a half miles. And yes, McGarvey says she also waxed floors, took Q-tips to the windows, and endured room inspections. "It's an attention to detail that carries over to everything," she explains. "If you take care of things like polishing your shoes, you'll take care of the ship."

57

A military career can be a great way for lawyers to get involved in government work. "I always had an interest in being an international attorney," says Capt. David Hayes of the Navy Judge Advocate General's Office. "When I coupled a legal practice in the navy with what I already knew about the navy, that was fascinating. . . . After nineteen months, I found myself on the island of Sardinia, starting to get a flavor for practicing law in an overseas environment." Hayes started out as a legal assistance attorney, dealing with military justice and civil law issues; he has overseen navy prosecutors, worked with the Pentagon's chief of operations, and eventually became chief of staff in the JAG office.

Working in so many different areas is typical of military jobs, Hayes says. "Provided you work hard and are successful, you can pretty much chart your own course," he says, adding that his work has run the gamut from helping sailors with landlord-tenant issues to figuring out how to conduct combat in Iraq. "I'm constantly challenged and that's one of the greatest things about our business," Hayes says. Plus, the diverse work experience that JAG attorneys get can help them transition into many different areas of private practice once their service in the military expires.

Since enlisting, McGarvey has also worked in a variety of positions. She has provided legal advice to sailors in civil matters; defended service members in criminal prosecutions from minor cases all the way to court-martial; and worked at Guantanamo and in Iraq. Now, she serves as the deputy executive assistant to the judge advocate general of the navy, reviewing documents before they reach the admiral for signature. McGarvey says each of her many navy jobs came with its own set of challenges—moving around a lot, for example.

MILITARY LAWYER: SOME SUBSPECIALTIES

- Offering legal assistance to soldiers
- Homeland security
- Courts-martial and military prosecutions
- Defending soldiers in civil and criminal matters
- International military law and strategy
- Admiralty law
- Environmental law

McGarvey says one of the best things about being a military attorney is being able to get diverse, meaningful work. "In some ways, the work that I've been involved in has a broader impact," she believes. "It runs the gamut. You never know what's coming next." McGarvey says she likes moving around a lot, meeting new people, and seeing new places; though constantly moving can be a challenge, it also keeps her work interesting. Hayes says being adventurous and willing to be challenged by new experiences daily are essential qualifications for the job. "I've seen the world; I've met some of the most interesting people that you can imagine; and I've tackled some of the most interesting issues you can imagine," he says. "If you want adventure, if you want challenge, if you want to make a difference every day . . . this is for you."

MILITARY LAWYER: BREAK-IN TIP

As for getting started, McGarvey recommends researching all of the different branches, as each service offers slightly different opportunities for attorneys and JDs. Each branch has its own operations for enlisting, training, and getting started in a military attorney career—find out more by visiting the resources listed at the end of this chapter. According to Hayes, the quality of applicants is getting better; he says he looks for high academic and extracurricular performance in candidates.

Despite all of his worldly experiences, Hayes says the most rewarding part of his job is still in helping young sailors with legal challenges and training new navy attorneys. "The day you put on this uniform, you become a leader," he says. And much of the way of thinking that helps on the job comes from Hayes's legal education, he says. "Getting a JD degree trains our minds to think in a certain way," Hayes explains. "We're regarded and respected as an officer who can generally do anything. We can look at very complex issues and distill them down into very concise points. We can articulate well both orally and in writing."

McGarvey cherishes the opportunity she has to serve her country and use her law degree at the same time. "For me, the navy ended up being a great fit because we do a lot of criminal law, international law, and operational law," McGarvey explains. "My law degree helps me because we are straight-out lawyers."

Criminal Justice Career Options for JDs

For the past five years, Jorge Montes has served as chairman of the Illinois Prisoner Review Board in Springfield and is the youngest chairman the board has ever had. After graduating law school in 1988, Montes began his career as a prosecutor specializing in civil enforcement actions, including child support enforcement. A journalism major in college, Montes then transitioned into a writer position, editing the ABA journal *Passport*. In 1994, he was appointed by the Illinois attorney general to serve as a spokesperson, often covering press releases and press conferences in criminal areas, such as consumer fraud. That same year, he was appointed as a member of the Prisoner Review Board and served in that position under three governors before becoming the chairman.

Montes says much of his workday is spent being present in the community. Since his tenure as chairman, he says, "it's become a much more community-friendly board." As a first-generation immigrant, Montes says he also brings a different worldview to the board; for instance, the board's voice mail and website are now bilingual, as are many of its forms.

"I very much enjoy determining new policies for the board," Montes says. Montes oversees a fifteen-member board that handles seven different types of hearings; he works with the legislature, the governor's office, and the public. As chairman, the brunt of his work centers on implementing new policies and overseeing long-term operations, though he still presides over all clemency hearings. By contrast, board members handle daily hearings. "On a day-to-day basis, most board members are zigzagging around the state, holding hearings in different penal institutions," Montes explains.

The most rewarding part of Montes's job is also the most challenging: engineering change. "What makes it challenging is the pressure that I get," he says. "It's a strictly political job." For starters, Montes says he serves at the will of the governor; plus, various groups lobby to institute new policies for the board—for instance, law enforcement agencies may lobby for stricter measures when they view some new policies as "going soft."

Jobs in criminal justice are plentiful, and they can cover a wide array of career options. Montes encourages law graduates to explore them. "Remain open to different possibilities; let your law degree serve as a springboard into incredible, different possibilities," he says. "You never know where an open mind can take you."

CRIMINAL JUSTICE CAREERS: SOME SUBSPECIALTIES

- Parole and probation careers
- Criminal defense organizations
- State and local police; other law enforcement careers
- Jobs in homeland security
- Careers with government entities, such as the FBI, the Department of Justice, and the Bureau of Prisons
- Careers in corrections and the prison system

Attorney Robert Meyers works in a different criminal justice job: as a New York State Police major who's in command of the New York State Thruway, from the Bronx line to Buffalo. With four hundred troopers under his direction, Meyers makes personnel decisions, works closely with the Thruway Authority, manages overtime, implements safety initiatives, and handles contracts and union paperwork. He is also involved in highway police work, particularly the decision-making process, such as setting up checkpoints and overseeing protocol for traffic stops.

Hired as a state trooper at age twenty-three, Meyers has worked his way through college, a master's degree, and then law school at night, getting financial assistance from his department. Meyers says he first thought about going to law school as a trooper, when he prosecuted his own traffic tickets in court. He says in his experience, most policemen with a JD join the force first and then end up going to law school.

CRIMINAL JUSTICE CAREERS: BREAK-IN TIP

Montes credits his "quasi-criminal" experience as a civil prosecutor for helping him land his current position. He encourages law graduates to consider all the different sides of criminal justice if they are interested in the field. Montes stresses the importance of having various criminal justice agencies work together, regardless of the ideologies they hold and the people they represent. "We should be interested in bringing everybody to the table," he says. "We are in need of people who can bridge the gap; people who work both sides."

The JD degree gives a level of credibility and promotes critical thinking on the job, Meyers says. "The JD has certainly made me aware of language; I read things much more closely," he says. Plus, "you need tremendous verbal skills to deescalate situations; to understand that people do have rights, even the criminals." Through his legal education, Meyers says he's become more aware of civil and constitutional rights. In investigations and police work, "you can step back and say 'let's make sure we're doing this correctly,'" he explains. Meyers says his law degree also helps during personnel investigations, particularly as he conducts interviews with complainants and takes the statements of troopers.

"If you come on any police department with a JD, you'll have the opportunity to advance through the organization," Meyers believes. "Having a JD gives you a leg up over other people in the same field."

Career Options in Legal Ethics and Professional Responsibility

In the field of legal ethics, it's often said that lawyers are a self-policing profession. Through state bar associations and their corresponding ethics boards, members are kept in check by having to adhere to a certain set of ethics—codes of conduct to which members of a profession subscribe—and being dealt penalties for noncompliance. Of course, someone needs to do the policing. Usually, the job falls on state bar counsel or another ethics enforcement officer.

Because ethics jobs generally require legal experience and can be few and far between, some ethics careers are begun on a volunteer basis. Donald Lundberg, for example, started his career in the world of legal ethics as a volunteer for the Indiana State Bar Association's Legal Ethics Committee. Working as a civil legal services attorney at the time, Lundberg says he became involved in legal ethics both out of personal interest and the internal needs of his organization. His interest evolved. After nine years of volunteer work, when the bar's ethics attorney left, Lundberg applied to fill the position. After a series of interviews—including with the disciplinary commission and the state supreme court's justices—Lundberg was selected. He has served in the position since 1991.

"I am the chief administrator and chief counsel for our office, which operates in two capacities: to screen and investigate claims of lawyer misconduct, and to charge and prosecute lawyer misconduct cases," Lundberg explains. As part of his job, Lundberg oversees a staff of lawyers, law clerks, and support staff; he also addresses questions about legal ethics and frequently speaks to lawyers' groups about ethical topics.

Lundberg enjoys "feeling that we're doing good work," he says. He recalls one disciplinary case against a well-established attorney in a local community who had taken control of an elderly client's assets, essentially misappropriating all of the woman's money in the end. "She was, I think, because of her age and failing health a very vulnerable person," Lundberg recounts, "and he took advantage of that vulnerability." Eventually, the attorney was disbarred.

Lundberg says ethics attorneys face some challenges and misconceptions—particularly when it comes to how they are viewed by their fellow attorneys. "There is a perception that people working in the discipline sometimes dislike lawyers," Lundberg explains. "We are always seen as 'the police,' in part because we are," he says, adding that being viewed as an enforcer often colors his relationships with his peers—after all, he is ultimately the guy who could hold his colleagues liable in a professional matter. "I love lawyers," says Lundberg. "Part of the reason I do this work is [that] I want the profession to be better."

Lundberg says that most ethics lawyers tend to have considerable experience before entering the field—though the type of experience that they bring to the table varies greatly. So does the experience needed for the job. For instance, Lundberg says lawyers working in ethics litigation must have top trial skills. On the other hand, those working in an investigative capacity must pay attention to detail, possess good problem-solving and analytical skills, have an understanding of what is provable and admissible at trial, and have "the instincts and creativity for knowing where to go to find the facts," Lundberg says.

LEGAL ETHICS CAREERS: BREAK-IN TIP

Lundberg recommends that interested attorneys expose themselves to the field of ethics as much as possible. Law firm ethics committees and state or local bar association ethics committees are some ideal ways to get started, "so that you are starting to think about legal ethics problems on a regular basis," he says. "Are you interested in actually doing it [daily]?" Lundberg recommends being flexible and willing to do different tasks when getting started in an ethics position—for example, doing some investigative work even if your primary interest is in litigation. "The more flexibility you bring to trying to get into this kind of work, the more likely it is that there'll be a slot for you," he says.

For lawyers working professional responsibility careers, ethics are at the forefront. "My hope is that lawyers are . . . always in the back of their minds thinking what their ethical responsibilities are," he says.

THERE'S MORE ON THE WEB!
Career Resources for This Chapter

ABA Section of Government and Public Sector Lawyers, http://www.abanet.org/govpub/

ABA Section of State and Local Government Law, http://www.abanet.org/statelocal/home.html

ABA Section of Public Contract Law, http://www.abanet.org/contract/home.html

The federal government's official jobs website, http://www.usajobs.gov/

National District Attorneys Association, http://www.ndaa.org/

National Association of Attorneys General, http://www.naag.org/

Judge Advocates Association, http://www.jaa.org/

Navy Judge Advocate General's Corps, http://www.jag.navy.mil/

Army Judge Advocate General's Corps, http://www.jagcnet.army.mil/

Judge Advocate General of the U.S. Air Force, http://hqja.jag.af.mil/

Marine Corps Judge Advocate, http://officer.marines.com/page/Officer-Law.jsp

Public Lawyer, trade magazine published by the ABA Section of Government and Public Sector Lawyers, http://www.abanet.org/govpub/pubs.html

Urban Lawyer, quarterly publication of the ABA Section of State and Local Law, http://www.abanet.org/statelocal/urbanlawyer/abstracts.html#currentissue1

Prosecutor, published by the National District Attorneys Association, http://www.ndaa.org/publications/ndaa/toc_prosecutor.html

Federal Legal Employment Opportunities Guide, published by NALP, the ABA Section of Government and Public Sector Lawyers, and the Partnership for Public Service, http://www.pslawnet.org/assets/397_0708fedlegalempguide.pdf

American Prosecutors Research Institute, http://www.ndaa.org/apri/index.html

National Criminal Justice Association, http://www.ncja.org//AM/Template.cfm?Section=Home

American Correctional Association, http://www.aca.org/

ABA Criminal Justice Section, http://www.abanet.org/crimjust/home.html

American Probation and Parole Association, http://www.appa-net.org/

Criminal Justice Magazine, published by the ABA Criminal Justice Section, http://www.abanet.org/crimjust/cjmag/22-4/home.html

Association of Professional Responsibility Lawyers, http://www.aprl.net/

National Organization of Bar Counsel, http://www.nobc.org/default.asp

ABA Center for Professional Responsibility, http://www.abanet.org/cpr/

National Council of Lawyer Disciplinary Boards, http://www.ncldb.org/

Professional Lawyer, published by the ABA Center for Professional Responsibility, http://www.abanet.org/cpr/pubs/proflaw.html

CHAPTER 4

Careers in
Academia and
Education

Though they represent just a minuscule part of open positions for JDs (typically reported as between 1 and 2 percent, depending on which study or survey is used), jobs in education and academia are available to those who are interested. JDs work in law schools, colleges and universities, primary and secondary schools, school district offices, libraries, research firms, and continuing legal education settings—both as educators and administrators. And for those working in education and academia, the field presents a fulfilling and rewarding way to put their legal education to use.

Read on for personal stories of success in education and academia.

Professor, Instructor, or Adjunct Professor

Though not often a starter job, teaching becomes a viable choice for many lawyers who are looking for a career change. Whether teaching a course to law students or tutoring college students on LSAT preparation, opportunities in teaching are plentiful.

"I had never considered teaching until I participated in the Academic Skills Program as a Dean's Scholar while I was a student," says Beth Wilson Hill, who teaches Advocacy at Pace Law School in New York. As an Academic Skills mentor, Hill assisted first-year students in organized study groups, focusing on legal analysis and exam preparation.

"Years later, I would run into students I had mentored and they would thank me and tell me that I helped them get through their first year of law school," she recalls.

Just a few years after graduating, Hill helped develop and began teaching an intense bar preparation course at her alma mater. The school contacted Hill when the curriculum committee voted to include the new bar preparation course, and she came to her interview well prepared—in fact, she turned the interview into a presentation, detailing course materials, assignments, and even what time the course should be offered. "The course I am offering focuses on organizing, analyzing, and writing in a clear and concise manner," she says, adding that she enjoys helping her students with the biggest exam of their lives and is happy to see schools recognize that they should assist students with bar preparation. "Taking the bar exam can be one of the most stressful periods in a person's life," Hill says. "You really get to know your students as you help them navigate through the process. I counsel them on applying for special accommodations, help them decide if they should postpone taking the exam, and give advice on rearranging their lives for a few months to accommodate the intense study schedule that they will need to adhere to in order to pass the bar exam."

But law schools are not the only avenues of employment for those interested in teaching: Colleges, universities, community colleges, and trade schools can also present attorneys with teaching opportunities. In particular, legal studies and paralegal programs; history, politics and government courses; and prelaw advising can be a great fit for those with a JD.

Judith Pollock Ciampi is a professor and coordinator of the paralegal program at Northern Essex Community College in Lawrence, Massachusetts. Ciampi says she enjoys the ever-changing nature of the work, seeing new students and often teaching new courses every semester. "You are always learning something new," she notes, "to stay up with the new developments in the areas in which you teach and to be prepared to answer student questions."

Ciampi spent two years honing her research and writing skills as a clerk for the New Hampshire Supreme Court, then worked as a corporate attorney for years before becoming an adjunct instructor and easing into teaching. She first taught a law school writing course. "After about ten years as a corporate attorney and five years as an adjunct instructor, I found that I enjoyed the academic pursuit of legal knowledge more than the actual practice of law," she states. After four years of teaching in the community college's paralegal program, Ciampi was hired part-time as a staff associate to help coordinate the program, then a year later took over coordinator duties full time.

Ciampi says her JD is useful in her teaching position, not only in the substantive knowledge she needs to teach legal studies, but also in being more organized in her thinking and writing. Plus, she says she often thinks back to her teachers and professors, assessing what she liked and disliked about their teaching methods and then using some of the techniques that worked well.

PROFESSOR/ADJUNCT PROFESSOR: SOME SUBSPECIALTIES

- Law school courses
- College-level legal studies courses
- Paralegal programs
- Other legal staff programs
- Bar exam preparation
- LSAT and law school preparation
- Legal writing help
- Substantive legal tutoring
- Prelaw advising

For those interested in teaching law students, who they know may be just as important as what they know. "Stay in touch with your professors from law school," recommends Hill. "They often know about upcoming opportunities at the law school and you can use them as references." Hill says being published in one's field can also be useful for landing a teaching job. In addition to knowledge of the subjects that one teaches, being enthusiastic about teaching is also essential. "When you really believe that what you are teaching is important, it shows," she says.

Of course, teaching is not without its challenges. Full-time teaching positions are generally hard to get, especially right out of law school, and an increasing number of colleges and law schools are looking for teaching experience before hiring anyone full-time. "Be prepared to adjunct for years," says Ciampi. "Full-time opportunities are difficult to come by." For those who ultimately want to teach full-time, Ciampi recommends getting started as an adjunct and then getting actively involved with college activities, such as conferences, professional development, even overseeing student club activities. Faculty who stay visible and get involved are more likely to be asked to come back and maybe even land a full-time position, Ciampi explains.

ADJUNCT PROFESSOR: BREAK-IN TIP

When Luz Carrion wanted to teach, she decided to take matters into her own hands: She proposed a new paralegal course in health law and was hired by Ciampi to develop and teach it. (See more about Carrion in Chapter 1, in the section about health law.) Ciampi says a great way to get started as an adjunct is to offer to teach a course in your area of expertise. Check academic offerings at colleges and law schools in your area to see if there are any gaps you could fill, then develop a proposal for a new course and send it to the administrator in charge. "The easiest way to carve out a niche for yourself is to identify new and emerging areas of law. Otherwise, you are competing with people who may have twenty-plus years of experience in a particular area of law," agrees Hill. "Think outside the box. Write a proposal for a new class and ask for an opportunity to present it. Review the school's course offerings and make sure that your proposed course is unique. Include as many details as possible in your proposal." Though requirements may vary by educational institution, your proposal should generally include a description of the course, a syllabus if possible, an overview of the topics you intend to teach, reasons why there will be demand for your course among students, and an explanation of why you are the right person to teach the class.

One common misconception is that teaching jobs are easy, netting professors a full-time paycheck for part-time hours. Not so, explains Ciampi. "Although your schedule is flexible, prep time and correcting time require many more hours than you anticipate, often on nights and weekends," she says. Plus, teaching jobs generally pay less than many other positions for JDs, including practicing law. Still, teaching brings more flexibility and at least some of the work can be done from home. Hill says her teaching job, coupled with her full-time job, makes for one long day. She says she often goes to Pace right from the office to teach in the evenings.

Depending on where one teaches, the academic level of students can also pose challenges, Ciampi says. The average college student is different from the average law student; two-year college courses often have students from various backgrounds and with various academic abilities. Ciampi says she's taught everyone from the eighteen-year-old who's fresh out of high school to the adult learner with years of experience in the legal field. That means a particular teaching environment may not work for everyone, Ciampi warns; she suggests that adjuncts ease into teaching and try out different places before committing to one school full time. For example, if teaching law students proves too intense, try undergraduate courses.

But the job's rewards clearly outweigh its challenges for many dedicated professors. Ciampi cites the opportunity to see people of all ages learn and grow academically and the satisfaction of helping people advance their careers as the most rewarding parts of her job. "When the students actually get what you're teaching and you can actually see growth and progress," she says, that's very gratifying.

Ciampi adds that she also gets great satisfaction from the emails and phone calls of successful former students—such as the ones who swear by using the same litigation notebook that they had put together as paralegal students. She recalls one student, Ana, who was determined to complete the paralegal program despite personal obstacles. She tried three times before she was successful. Ciampi encouraged the student to continue the program and helped guide her to a successful legal career— an achievement that was apparent when Ciampi watched Ana receive one of the college's awards for alumni. "Ana still calls and emails me periodically to update me on her plans and accomplishments," Ciampi says. "She still remembers what I told her about dealing with difficult times and has shared the mantra 'this too shall pass' with others. She has taught me that patience and small words of encouragement mean more to students than one might think."

Hill says she likes teaching an elective, as she finds that her students actually want to be in class and are grateful for her instruction. She also enjoys hearing from students who reap the benefits of her teaching. "I love the fact that I get tangible results from teaching the class—seeing my students pass the bar exam," she says. "I think that I am almost as excited and nervous as my students on the day that the results are released."

Though it is a satisfying career, teaching is not for everyone. "Teaching is something that you should only do because you really want to," Hill says. "Students deserve to have teachers who care about their students and are passionate about what they teach."

Law School Administrator

Like law firms, law schools don't run themselves. Besides teaching positions, law school administration can be a viable alternative for those with a law degree and a field in which people can help and touch just as many students' lives as those in teaching positions.

Carol Q. O'Neil started out in law school administration after practicing in the corporate tax field. When she learned that one of her former first-year professors at Georgetown Law Center was heading up the search committee for a new assistant dean for the JD program, O'Neil applied—approaching her alma mater, a strategy that many law school administrators say is a great way to get started in the field.

In that position, O'Neil worked with students and faculty on the school's curriculum, staying at Georgetown for seventeen years now. As associate dean of academic administration, O'Neil oversees curriculum planning, the registrar's office, and adjunct faculty. She also chairs the school's curriculum and academic standards committee, which considers new courses and new programs, such as a program for first-years who work on transnational legal problems.

LAW SCHOOL ADMINISTRATOR: SOME AVENUES OF EMPLOYMENT

Different law schools have different procedures and employ administrators in various subsets. Here are some examples to consider:

- Academics
- Curriculum planning, design, strategy, or review
- Clinical education
- Career services
- Admissions
- Recruiting and outreach
- Pro bono or public interest work
- Financial aid
- Joint degree programs
- International programs
- Residence life
- Student affairs

For O'Neil, the most rewarding part of the job is helping faculty and "working with faculty on what they want to teach and any teaching issues," she says. The job's biggest challenge for her is balancing the differing needs of students, faculty, and the administration.

O'Neil says her organizational ability and attention to detail serve her well. She also cites the ability not to react personally to criticism as essential in the field—law school administrators, she explains, receive comments and suggestions from faculty and students frequently and must be able to listen and take positive steps based on those comments. There's a perception that law school administration is unduly bureaucratic and not intellectually engaging, but O'Neil says there are many opportunities for intellectual engagement for anyone working in a law school environment. Many schools hire "career" administrators, but at some schools, administrators also get to teach a limited number of courses, seminars, or clinics.

LAW SCHOOL ADMINISTRATOR: BREAK-IN TIP

O'Neil says "anyone who's in administration needs a basic interest and familiarity with what's going on in the legal education community." She recommends reading histories of legal education and trade journals such as the *Journal of Legal Education*. In addition, O'Neil says one way to get your foot in the door is by mentoring students or others, or participating in student organizations in a role that allows you to run things, which is essentially what administrators do.

For those with a love of the law school experience and education, a career as a law school administrator may be a great fit, allowing them to shape legal education and touch the lives of students and faculty alike.

Legal Career Services

A subset of law school administration is legal career services. Career professionals advise law students and alumni on finding a job, entering a particular field, and preparing for their professional lives after law school.

Ann Griffin took a job as a staff attorney at a large immigration firm after graduating from the University of Detroit Mercy, School of Law. "I had a sense that practicing would not be my be-all-end-all, but wanted to try it," she says. After a couple of years, Griffin returned to her alma mater to teach legal research and writing, and then three years later transitioned into a position in admissions and student affairs. "I liked it, but it was not my calling," Griffin says, so she actively pursued a career services position at the school—and landed one when her predecessor left in 2000.

Now assistant dean of career services and outreach, Griffin offers individual attention and counseling to students and alumni of the law school. She also spends time on employer development: looking for opportunities for students, programming, and researching the legal market. Many of her tasks and responsibilities depend on what time of the year it is, she says; her job revolves around the school year and the recruiting schedule. One challenge is to "provide something for everybody," Griffin says. "Our challenge is to make sure that students can come to us and should come to us no matter what their interests are."

Louis Thompson started out in career services after first practicing as a products liability litigator and then taking on a federal court clerkship. "It was during that time that I realized that. . . . I loved dealing with people, reading, and writing," Thompson says. When an associate dean of career services position opened up at Thompson's alma mater, Temple University Beasley School of Law, Thompson applied. "It didn't look like I had any [of the] qualifications, but I thought I brought other things to the table and applied anyway," he says. It worked—Thompson landed the position, and he now makes it a point to teach other law grads a lesson he learned in the process: It's important not to count yourself out before you even submit a résumé!

At Temple, Thompson provides individual counseling, helping students with résumés and career plans; he says his office sees five hundred to six hundred students per year. Thompson also gives many presentations and puts together programs on everything from on-campus interviewing to job selection; he tracks down speakers and handles related event planning. Part of Thompson's job is to keep track of student and alumni employment data and manage related reporting. He contacts alumni to find out about their employment, tracks alumni work, and maintains related databases. But just as important is Thompson's marketing function: In addition to students, Thompson keeps in close contact with law firms and other legal employers, sometimes cold-calling firms to line up possible interviews and prospects.

To work in legal career services, "you absolutely have to have good people skills," says Thompson. "Unless someone likes you and is willing to be honest with you and trust you, you're not going to be able to help them as best as you can." Career services professionals also need to know their market, says Thompson, including all of the different employers and work environments in which JDs can work.

Thompson adds that he's learned a lot about the many things JDs can do since starting his position. Part of the reason why Griffin finds her job fulfilling is just that opportunity to let them know about different career options. She says she was a student "with her head in the sand" in law school, and says law school is a great time to learn and experience new things.

LEGAL CAREER SERVICES: BREAK-IN TIP

One doesn't need a full-time position to get started in career services. For example, some people begin by volunteering on their law firms' recruiting committees. "A lot of people do career services on an informal basis," says Thompson, like introducing candidates to possible employers or referring colleagues to job openings. "Every time you have an opportunity to do that, do so," Thompson advises.

Naturally, those who work in career services find it most rewarding when they help a student land a fulfilling job prospect. "Sometimes you don't even realize you're helping people," says Thompson. During one event, he recalls talking to a judge about an intern whose résumé Thompson sent over. The judge raved about her work, and was overheard by a lawyer at a small firm, who then inquired whether the intern had a job. The judge asked the intern to call the firm, and a week later, Thompson got an email from the intern informing him that she got the job and thanking him for making such a difference in her life.

Griffin says she keeps students' thank-you notes on her bulletin board as a reminder of the difference she makes in students' lives. "I absolutely love hearing from students that they've landed a job and they enjoy it," she says. "It's also fun to watch students develop and grow and learn over time."

School Superintendent or Administrator

Colleges and law schools are not the only viable places of employment for law graduates. Some JDs work at public or private primary and secondary schools, public school districts, and school superintendents' offices—teaching law or working in school administration.

Michael Magone taught junior high school for two years before going to law school, picking the law degree over other graduate programs because of its versatility. After practicing for two years, Magone found

73

that he missed education and went back to teach school law at the high school level. With his interest and experience in both education and law, Magone decided to move into school administration and took a position as a high school principal, eventually becoming the K–8 superintendent in Missoula, Montana, and finally moving into his current position as superintendent of the Lolo School District in Lolo, Montana.

"Being in a K–8 school district, I'm more of a jack-of-all-trades," Magone says. In addition to working with the school board, being in charge of school district administration, and overseeing the hiring and dismissal process, Magone sometimes helps out in the "trenches," like filling in for the crossing guard or supervising students on the playground at recess!

Magone says his legal background offers him the opportunity to spot potential issues in advance. "I know enough to recognize issues and seek help in advance," he says. Like many other JDs in nonpracticing positions, Magone also hails the critical and analytical thinking skills he picked up in law school.

One challenge in stepping back into education after practicing law for a few years lies in first getting used to the confidence level and adversarial thinking that attorneys have, then having to shed that when transitioning into a nonpracticing position, Magone says. "As an attorney, you've got a pretty high confidence level," he explains. "You're used to working in a certain fashion in an adversarial environment. . . . When you step back into the educational arena that can be hurtful [because] people can be threatened by that." Magone is right: According to a study cited in the *National Law Journal,* attorneys are competitive, adversarial, and less likely to collaborate than people in other occupations. Though the profession may not need a study to know that, the point of the article is significant for JDs seeking nontraditional occupations.

CAREERS AT K–12 SCHOOLS: BREAK-IN TIP

Magone says most people get started in school administration after teaching for a while and wanting some additional responsibilities, challenges, or income. Some JDs opt to teach K–12 students, and Magone says that classes in law, social studies, or history are particularly good fits for those with a JD and a passion for teaching. He adds that he proposed a course on legal issues and current events when he first went back to education. The course started out with just five kids and soon ballooned into two sections with thirty kids each.

When Magone decided to leave the practice of law and go back to education, he says many people—not just friends and family, but also colleagues in both fields—questioned his decision. But for Magone his contribution to the community and school district, coupled with the satisfaction he gets from being involved in his students' lives, keeps his career rewarding. And teaching with a JD can be a gateway to even more career opportunities. For example, Magone went back to school and recently obtained his doctorate in education and plans to slowly take on educational consulting projects. "Follow your passion," Magone says. "That's what is most important."

Law Librarian

It's no secret that the law is a research-driven profession—and some JDs choose to make research their calling and profession. Law librarians help attorneys, legal staff, and others research legal issues, find the law, and figure out answers to legal questions.

Ann Fessenden started working as a law librarian after graduating from college, went back to obtain her master's in library science degree, and then finally got her law degree attending school at night while working as a full-time law librarian at her law school. Now the circuit librarian at the U.S. Court of Appeals in St. Louis, Missouri, Fessenden started out working in reference and acquisitions. She currently manages the court's law library, overseeing personnel, budgeting, and planning. She also serves as president of the American Association of Law Libraries.

While some law librarians—particularly those at smaller libraries where resources and staff are more scarce—tend to do a little bit of everything, others choose to specialize. For example, Fessenden says some may focus on reference, assisting patrons directly, while others may oversee the library's acquisitions or catalog; still other law librarians may specialize in technological or electronic services.

LAW LIBRARIAN: SOME EMPLOYERS AND LIBRARY TYPES

- Law schools
- Private law firms
- State courts
- County courts
- Federal courts
- Corporate law departments

The most challenging part of the job is keeping up with constant changes, Fessenden says. "Delivery methods and the way we do research have been changing so fast," she explains. Along with that, Fessenden says there's also a challenge "trying to make our users understand the ways that we're still needed" and educating people about the role of the law library and its librarians in an age of dependence on online research providers.

As in any other nonpracticing legal career, the JD can be helpful. "It helps you understand the subject matter and terminology," Fessenden says. "You understand how it all fits together. If you have to figure out what a tort is when somebody's asking, it slows you down a lot." Having a JD also "puts the librarian on a more equal footing," Fessenden says, pointing out that at law schools, many law librarians also serve as faculty. Still, an MLS degree is also critical to law librarianship, she says, "because you have to know how a library works. The library has gotten more complicated. You need a foundation."

LAW LIBRARIAN: BREAK-IN TIP

"We do have a lot of refugees," says Fessenden, as some law librarians enter the field after practicing and realizing it's not what they want to do. Others discover their knack for research in law school, such as in a research and writing class or while talking to a law librarian. If you're interested in law librarianship, Fessenden recommends a part-time job or internship to try the field on for size. She says organizational skills and "being able to think of things in hierarchical ways" can be helpful in the field. Even more important are people skills. "You have to be service oriented," says Fessenden, as "you're going to be in a service role." Teaching experience or skills can also help, as many law librarians end up teaching in formal or informal environments, whether it's instructing a research course or mentoring patrons on their research skills.

"Be open to different possibilities," Fessenden recommends, particularly when it comes to the various settings and environments in which law librarians work. She recalls that she first came to the court of appeals with the intention of getting some administrative experience then transitioning back into law school libraries within a few years—yet twenty years later, she is still there. "I like being part of the administration of

76

justice," says Fessenden. "You work with intelligent, well-educated people. You do interesting things [and] the research can be fascinating."

Educational Consultant

Steven Roy Goodman is putting his JD to interesting use: As an educational consultant, Goodman advises students on college admissions and serves as an admissions strategist for students and their families. Goodman says he's always had a love for college and university admissions; he has a master's degree in education, wrote a law school dissertation on class-based discrimination in college admissions, and started his practice while he was still in law school. Goodman is also the author of *College Admissions Together: It Takes a Family* (Capital Books, 2007).

For Goodman, the most fulfilling part of the job is playing a pivotal role in helping students find the right fit in a college, including helping with self-exploration, he says. The most challenging part of the work comes from managing unreasonable expectations, says Goodman, like with students who are gunning for a college that is out of their league.

EDUCATION LAW: SOME SUBSPECIALTIES

Some education lawyers advise clients—whether they be students, municipalities, school districts, educators, or others—on subjects dealing with school law. On its website, the Education Law Association lists the following topics of discussion at its annual conference:

- Affirmative action
- First Amendment (speech issues, press, religion, assembly, dress codes)
- Fourth Amendment search/seizure
- Due process
- Equal protection
- The No Child Left behind Act
- Reauthorization of IDEA (Individuals with Disabilities Education Act)
- Educational issues of international interest
- Legal issues affecting community colleges
- Legal issues concerning technology
- Rights of special needs students
- Impact on student records and privacy
- Employment discrimination
- Sexual harassment

Whether advising clients on legal matters in school law or other educational concerns such as admissions, educational consulting can be a natural match for JDs, who come out of law school with great analytical and communication skills. Goodman says his legal education also helps him better understand and apply ethical boundaries in his consulting business, particularly when clients want something unethical—for instance, when a parent asks him to write a student's essay or offers a large sum in exchange for a guarantee that the student will get into a particular school. "I understand how it's really important to be clear about what I do and offer, and what I don't," Goodman explains.

He adds that law school helped him understand and pinpoint the exact specialty he wanted to pursue in his educational career. "It helped me recognize my strengths and weaknesses in my own thinking," says Goodman. "In thinking about how I wanted to run my practice, what services I wanted to offer, the law degree helped me see the limits and opportunities."

EDUCATION CONSULTANT: GETTING STARTED

Goodman is a prime example of someone who has taken his law degree and legal education and turned it into a successful nonlegal career. "Don't be afraid to follow your passion," he advises. "Being a lawyer is very prestigious in our society. Sometimes, it's difficult to explain to [someone] that you're going to give up the law." Still, Goodman—along with many others—says it's essential for law grads to follow their passions and work in an environment that best fits their interests and career goals—whether that be in the legal field or not. "The JD is a versatile degree because it tells a future employer that this person has gone through the rigor of being able to survive the JD curriculum," says Goodman. "The employer knows that this is a student who can stick with something."

"It's really important to find what you like, do it, and do a lot of it," Goodman believes. "I'm a huge fan of forging your own path. Life is happier when you do that."

Legal Research Company Representative

Heidi Bloedow didn't know what she wanted to do upon graduating law school, but she did know she didn't want to practice law. With seven years of experience working alongside doctors and patients in the medical field, Bloedow also knew she enjoyed tending to customers and helping people.

Through word of mouth, Bloedow heard about a job opening that would allow her to use her customer service skills as well as her new law degree, and she became a reference attorney at Thomson West. In that position, Bloedow assisted attorneys and others with their questions about researching on Westlaw, the company's computerized legal research database. She helped formulate search queries; sometimes, she would simply serve to reassure customers who have tried everything to research a possible query that nothing new was available.

Bloedow soon moved up in the ranks—she explains that Thomson typically promotes from within. Working with the company for ten years, she now serves as Thomson's director of reference attorneys and oversees the work and operations of seven managers and their teams of attorneys. Though Bloedow has been involved with many different aspects of the company's business—from product development to setting up call centers to training and consulting—she says she still enjoys getting phone calls and interacting with customers.

Being a reference attorney and helping people with their research questions is just one of the many positions available to JDs at legal research companies. Other career options exist in sales and marketing, editorial, account management, training, and product development. Bloedow says she's experienced much better work-life balance in her position at Thomson West than many of her peers at law firms, and she enjoys having a nonpracticing position while still getting the chance to use her legal education. "There's never a boring day," Bloedow says. "We take three thousand phone calls per day, so there is always something you've never heard of." Bloedow also points out that the business cycle is often

---

LEGAL RESEARCH COMPANIES: SOME CAREER OPTIONS

- Reference attorneys help customers with their research questions.
- Salespeople and marketing associates market the product to customers and potential customers.
- Account managers work with current customers and train their staff.
- Editorial managers write headnotes and other legal works or assist the company's authors.
- Product development associates help innovate and develop new products.

more predictable than the law firm environment and says her job has been more manageable than the competitive nature of the practice that some of her peers have experienced.

Naturally, stellar research skills are needed in reference attorney positions, and Bloedow says it can be helpful to understand not just how Westlaw works but also what the many different written sources—yes, actual books!—in the law library contain, and the purposes they serve. For example, Bloedow says understanding how secondary versus primary authority works can help reference attorneys better understand which online sources to use when helping customers. "Listening skills are critical," she says; "also, being able to ask the right questions." For instance, she says sometimes customers call after getting deeply invested in their research, which can make it hard for them to see broader issues—and reference attorneys have to be able to see through the customer's research and articulate issues in a simple format.

But equally important for the job are an understanding of the legal research company's business, Bloedow says, an awareness of current trends in the market, and a customer-oriented attitude. "Service is everything," she says. "If you're not good with people, this won't work for you." To learn about legal research, Bloedow says becoming a reference attorney is the best option. "There's no better way to learn our business than to be a reference attorney," she says. "You're on the product eight hours a day, helping people."

LEGAL RESEARCH COMPANY REPRESENTATIVE: BREAK-IN TIP

Bloedow got her start at Thomson West through word of mouth: She knew a Thomson employee and was called in to fill an opening. But she says another way to break into a career at a legal research company is to watch for postings on companies' websites, and call for an informational interview to learn more about different positions. Bloedow adds that work experience in virtually any field can be invaluable to getting hired. "When people have real-world experience, they just have a different perspective," she notes. "It's really about communication and being able to talk to people." Bloedow says she's interviewed hundreds of candidates over the years and is always amazed at how many new graduates limit their résumés to their legal experience and education only. She encourages law grads to apply to nonpracticing positions in general, and says they shouldn't discount nontraditional work for fear of appearing overqualified for a position.

Bloedow says she still enjoys the human interaction and customer service components of her job, and relishes when she gets phone calls—usually escalated ones—from customers who need help. "I learn every day, even in this role," says Bloedow. "We're always managing higher and higher customer expectations and always trying to look for new ways to move forward."

Professional Development or Continuing Legal Education Careers

Legal education doesn't end with the JD, and neither do educational career opportunities. Many JDs find a fulfilling career working in continuing legal education (CLE) or professional development. After all, most states have mandatory CLE requirements for lawyers, and law firms are increasingly paying attention to the training and professional development of their lawyers.

There are different avenues to work in CLE, explains Cheri Harris, executive director of CLEreg, a national trade association for CLE regulators headquartered in Indianapolis. Some CLE careers focus on regulation, making sure lawyers are fulfilling their annual CLE requirements; others work for CLE providers, including state associations, law schools, and nonprofit educational providers. Regulators, Harris says, generally deal with their state's CLE board or commission, which is the policy-making body; they oversee and decide on accreditation issues for CLE programs; and they ensure that attorneys are meeting their mandatory CLE requirements.

Harris really forged her own path in the field. She has worked in nonprofit and government settings since she graduated law school, including clerking for the Indiana chief justice, working for the state's legislature, and providing educational programs for state court judges at the Indiana Judicial Center. Harris was looking for a part-time nonprofit position at the same time that CLEreg was looking for an executive director, to be housed at the state of Indiana's CLE office; Harris submitted a proposal and was hired. She now manages the trade association, retaining and expanding membership, providing information to the public, and helping CLE providers who are interested in getting new courses or seminars accredited.

Lawrence Center is on the other side of the CLE spectrum. As executive director of CLE at Georgetown University Law Center in Washington, D.C., Center plans CLE programs—many of them national in scope—for attorneys and others. Center also had an extensive nonprofit background before starting his current position in 1985: He worked for a

81

nonprofit research firm that specialized in criminal law; provided crime prevention services to seniors; worked for the National Coalition for Jail Reform; and ran a master's-level legal studies program in Philadelphia.

PROFESSIONAL DEVELOPMENT OR CONTINUING LEGAL EDUCATION CAREERS: SOME EMPLOYERS

- State CLE offices
- Bar associations
- Trade associations
- Law firms (particularly large and midsize ones)
- Law schools
- Courts

For Center, the most fulfilling part of the job is creating innovative programs from the ground up, from the school's E-Discovery Institute to its Corporate Counsel Institute. "Building these kinds of programs from scratch is very rewarding," he says. "The law degree allows you in so many ways to give back to the legal community. . . . It allows me to try to help improve the quality of legal [education] and, frankly, to improve the cause of justice."

Center says his biggest challenge is competition: "Forty-two states have mandatory CLE," he says, "so CLE has become very big business." On the regulatory side, Harris says the sheer quantity of changes can make it hard to keep up. "People need more opportunities to be brought up to

---

PROFESSIONAL DEVELOPMENT OR CONTINUING LEGAL EDUCATION CAREERS: BREAK-IN TIP

When it comes to CLE regulation careers, "any additional background in education is helpful, [as is] a background in regulations or mediation," says Harris. She explains that regulators are often charged with "building bridges" between the state's regulatory body, CLE providers, and CLE participants who have to fulfill requirements. Center says flexibility, interpersonal communication skills, time management and prioritizing skills, and problem-solving skills are all necessary for CLE providers to have.

---

date than ever," she says, and new questions about CLE are popping up, with which CLE regulators must wrestle. For example, should in-house programs count toward mandatory CLE requirements? Should law office management courses? How about podcasts? Should ethics be a separate mandatory requirement? Should new attorneys participate in mandatory "bridge the gap" programs to impart technical and practical skills?

Careers in CLE and professional development can be a lucrative, if not very well known, alternative for JDs. "It's the kind of career that allows one to build and maintain knowledge in a variety of practice areas," says Center.

THERE'S MORE ON THE WEB!
Career Resources for This Chapter

The Association of American Law Schools, http://aals.org/
ABA Section of Legal Education and Admissions to the Bar, http://www.abanet.org/legaled/home.html
Society of American Law Teachers, http://www.saltlaw.org/
Education Law Association, http://www.educationlaw.org/
American Association for Paralegal Education, http://aafpe.org/
National Association of College and University Attorneys, http://www.nacua.org/
PreLaw Advisors National Council, http://www.planc.org/
American Association of School Administrators, http://www.aasa.org/
Journal of Legal Education, http://aals.org/resources_journal.php
Thomson/West, http://www.thomson.com/
Reed Elsevier/Lexis-Nexis, http://www.reed-elsevier.com/
Internet Legal Research Group, http://www.ilrg.com/
The Association for Continuing Legal Education, http://www.aclea.org/
Continuing Legal Education Regulators Association, https://www.clereg.org/
ABA Center for Continuing Legal Education, http://www.abanet.org/cle/home.html

---

CHAPTER 5

Positions in Law Office Management and Administration

Most JDs work in private practice, but law firms aren't just workplaces for attorneys. From managing the firm's operations to overseeing staff, from helping attorneys market their services to recruiting new talent, able law school graduates can find plenty of nonpracticing job opportunities. Many law firms specifically require a JD for upper-level management positions—not only do JDs understand the business of law and the practice of attorneys better than most non-JDs, but those in the field say that the law degree also imparts a certain respect and status, which can make it easier to chart a successful course in law firm management.

Read on for information about exciting careers in law office management and administration.

Law Firm Business Manager or Executive

Law firms don't run themselves. They require capable business managers to oversee the firm's day-to-day operations and long-term strategy.

As chief operating officer of Stinson Morrison Hecker, LLP, in Kansas City, Terry Brummer is responsible for all of the firm's business and strategic operations. Dealing with long-term prospects more so than day-to-day issues, Brummer says his role has evolved into strategic direction, overseeing mergers, lateral acquisitions, and practice group management. He has eight directors who report to him; he also oversees lateral searches, financial and personnel management, and marketing operations.

It took Brummer several career tracks to end up in law office management. After law school, Brummer practiced tax law and commercial litigation; he then served as executive director of a bar association in St. Louis, worked as a public defender in Missouri for seven years, and eventually ran the state's public defender system. "I realized after practicing for about seven years that I'm more interested in how things work," he says. "It was going to be important for me to specialize in something and I wasn't interested in specializing for my whole life in one area." Through a friend, Brummer heard about and landed a position in court management, then transferred into private law firm management, working for three different firms in the past twenty years.

Those diverse work experiences help Brummer manage others as the COO. He also has the right personality for the job: He says he's marketing-oriented, entrepreneurial, and more interested in the big picture than the minute details. "The most challenging part is balance," Brummer says. Most lawyers don't understand—or are too busy to deal with—management issues, Brummer explains, so for some, the task of balancing day-to-day management issues can be exacerbated by attorneys' lack of knowledge about the importance of law firm management.

Management skills and the ability to multitask are essential for a position in law firm management, Brummer says, as are strong organizational and time-management skills. Law firm managers must be able to identify and manage different personality types, figuring out what motivates them and how to lead them effectively, says Brummer. He recalls managing his firm through a large merger and says he enjoyed tackling the challenge—and the risk—of helping two large firms come together.

Brummer says generalists are more likely to succeed in law firm management than those who focus on a narrow subspecialty. "By necessity, you're going to have to touch everything," he explains. One exception? You might find a great career if you have honed a specialized skill set, such as technical skills or marketing skills, Brummer says.

Having a JD definitely helps, "if [in] nothing else, just having to talk the talk," Brummer says. "In a large law firm, if you're a lawyer, even if you're not practicing, you're still a member of the club." Understanding how lawyers are trained, how they think, and how they work is essential in law office administration, Brummer says—for example, he says that having experienced the pressures of billing his time makes him more understanding of other attorneys' drone work of having to put down their time every day.

A career in law firm management is rewarding, both financially and substantively. Brummer says his firm's partners see him as a valuable

---

LAW FIRM MANAGEMENT: BREAK-IN TIP

Typically, JDs enter the law office management field in one of two ways: They either gradually take on additional administrative responsibilities at the firms where they practice, or they have some management or business background before becoming attorneys and end up using that background to their advantage in law firm administration. "The easiest way to get in is at a smaller firm," Brummer says. "If you do have any business skills, there's a need that most law firms have [for law firm managers]. The law firm industry is so fertile for so many different areas of sophistication." It's important to note that law firm administration encompasses many different job titles and job descriptions. Some firms might have "office managers" or "administrators," for example, who oversee day-to-day operations, and "business managers" or "executives" to oversee long-term strategic direction. Therefore, read job postings carefully to make sure you're applying for a position that's the right fit for you—and vice versa.

---

player in the firm, who supports their practice and helps bring money to the firm. "There's so much variety," says Brummer. "What I really enjoy is the interaction with people in trying to get to a goal."

Manager of Recruiting

It's no secret that law firms are increasingly battling rising attrition rates; at the same time, the pressure is on for firms to hire the most qualified talent they can find. Many large and midsize firms don't just rely on outside legal recruiters to land new attorneys; rather, they hire a full-time recruiting manager or director to take care of the firm's hiring needs. That position can be filled by an able JD who chooses law office administration over practicing.

Michael Gotham serves as the manager of recruiting at Heller Ehrman, LLP, in San Francisco, overseeing firmwide recruitment efforts and programs and supervising seven recruiting managers and seven support staff. "I manage the overall recruiting process for the firm," Gotham explains, "establish[ing] policies, [and handling] recruiting systems [and] tools for hiring." He also approves any nonstandard offer terms and oversees the firm's on-campus recruiting schedule.

After graduating law school in 1993, Gotham spent two years as a litigation associate, then decided to look for nontraditional employment when he determined he no longer enjoyed the practice. He started as a temporary career services officer at a Seattle law school and was eventually offered the chance to become the school's director of career services. Legal career services were just getting popular across the nation, Gotham says; he spent five years at the school before deciding to move into law firm recruiting.

Gotham began as a recruiting manager—typically, this position entails more hands-on recruiting work, he explains: interviewing candidates, reviewing résumés, running the summer associate and call-back interview programs, and getting involved with new associate orientation. Gotham says he enjoyed on-the-ground recruiting and the close relationships he developed with associates through recruiting them, bringing them in, and then working with them; he says he often felt that he served as the bridge between new associates and the firm's management. In his current position, Gotham says the most rewarding part of the job is being able to create lasting systems and infrastructures and building teams with his managers.

Recruiters are the firm's most skilled interviewers," says Gotham. He cites people skills and the ability to "deal with a lot of different personalities within the law firm world" as some of the most important skills for the job. Plus, Gotham says recruiting managers must be able to "really intuit other people; have insight into folks and be able to spot answers that aren't quite right."

MANAGER OF RECRUITING: BREAK-IN TIP

Gotham says some law firm recruiters come in after working in career services at law schools. "It's easier for an attorney to get a job at a career services office than a law firm because law schools realize the value of that experience," he says. Gotham says more and more people are entering legal recruiting as a profession, and coming in with a better understanding of what recruiting entails.

Gotham says his JD degree is invaluable in his success as a legal recruiter. "You understand the language of the law; you can talk to [attorneys] about their practice," he explains. "You can evaluate résumés and people's experience better." Plus, a legal education translates into better analytical skills in any part of the legal profession, including issues with recruiting new talent. "You can really analyze issues and come to conclusions and present those conclusions to the attorneys," Gotham says.

Gotham is quick to clear up any misconceptions about legal recruiting being an "easy" alternative to the practice of law. "You work really hard in this profession," he says. "If you're truly committed, you'll work just as hard [as in practicing positions]."

Law Firm Marketing or Public Relations

"I'd always enjoyed writing," says John Tuerck, director of communications at Ropes & Gray, LLP, in Boston. In fact, Tuerck became a writer soon after graduating law school—and after a few years of practicing benefits and compliance law as corporate counsel for an investment company. He began his writing career at a suburban newspaper in Richmond, Virginia, covering the court beat; he soon landed a news editor position at the *Virginia Lawyers Weekly*. Tuerck worked on some high-profile cases, including the sniper attacks, he says, often explaining legal concepts to the mainstream press.

Soon, Tuerck realized that a fresh opportunity was presenting itself: handling writing and public relations at law firms. "I began to understand that law firms were getting more interested in public relations," he explains. Through networking with a newly appointed chief marketing officer, he transitioned into the law firm public relations world. In his current position, Tuerck fields requests from reporters, including daily newspapers, trade magazines, and electronic media. He handles the firm's writing and editing needs, writing marketing materials and press releases and placing bylined articles. Tuerck also oversees the firm's client alerts, which are regular notices of the firm's activities sent out to clients, as well as the firm's internal communications. "My primary overall responsibility is to get positive visibility for this law firm," he explains.

One challenge that comes with the position lies in "functioning at the speed of the media with the caution of a large law firm," Tuerck says. Cautious law firms like to mull over press opportunities, sometimes even taking media requests through various committees; with impending—sometimes same-day—deadlines, that can be tough to juggle.

The law degree proves valuable in law firm marketing and public relations: Tuerck says it reassures attorneys that he speaks the legal language and sometimes results in a higher level of respect. Because attorneys have high expectations, Tuerck says law firm communications professionals must learn to perform at a high level of quality.

Perhaps most importantly, Tuerck says public relations professionals must have "institutional knowledge," citing familiarity with the firm as the key to success. Tuerck says he attends practice group meetings and wades through the meetings' contents to find a good story, "always looking for fresh content, fresh insight, and fresh angles," he says.

LAW FIRM PUBLIC RELATIONS: SOME TYPICAL JOB DUTIES

- Responds to media requests and arranges interviews and other engagements with reporters and editors.
- Helps attorneys write and place bylined articles.
- Writes press releases, marketing materials, and other internal and eternal communications
- Oversees the firm's communications with the public and the media, and strives to present the firm in a positive light.

LAW FIRM MARKETING: SOME TYPICAL JOB DUTIES

Oversees the firm's marketing strategy, day-to-day marketing operations, long-term marketing plans, or all three.

- Assists with client retention, cross-services marketing to existing clients, and new client marketing efforts.
- Helps with business development.
- Seeks opportunities to increase visibility for the firm.
- Oversees firm advertising.
- May also take on the public relations duties described above.

For Tuerck, the most rewarding part of the job is not just being able to place great stories about the firm, but also showing reporters or editors a great story they may not have known about. He recalls one article that he pitched and placed successfully about the "aftermath" of his firm's merger. Tuerck started in his position just a month after his firm merged with another large firm; later, he thought it would be interesting to do a story that followed up on the merger. "I wanted to tell the world that it's actually worked out really well," he explains. "Does anybody ever do a follow-up [on firm mergers]?"

LAW FIRM MARKETING OR PUBLIC RELATIONS: BREAK-IN TIP

In public or media relations, writing skills and experience are essential. Tuerck says his five years of media experience have been absolutely invaluable in his current job; he says he understands how editors work and what their constraints are.

One thing is for sure: Despite any "industry obituaries" that may have been published in trade publications, legal marketing and public relations careers aren't about to go extinct. "I see it as a growing niche, at big law firms in particular," says Tuerck. He says law firms are becoming increasingly aware that marketing is a key function.

Law Firm Pro Bono Counsel

Some law firms are signaling their commitment to pro bono work by hiring an attorney or nonattorney director to oversee the firm's pro bono services. At Weil Gotshal & Manges, LLP, Miriam Buhl serves as pro bono counsel, directing the firm's pro bono efforts and coordinating the pro bono projects handled by its eleven hundred attorneys.

Among other duties, Buhl works with the firm's pro bono committee to set priorities and policies and reports to the committee on lawyers' pro bono performance; she also works with outside pro bono and legal aid organizations to develop connections and build relationships that result in pro bono referrals for the firm. Buhl screens pro bono cases that come in, interviews clients, and reviews requests for assistance; she also distributes pro bono matters, sets up supervision, and coordinates training. "There is so much to do—both day-to-day and 'big picture,'" she says. "As the firm grows, so must our pro bono footprint. I also worry a lot about reaching more people in need—how to do it."

Those who are interested in becoming pro bono counsel will be well served by honing their marketing, fund-raising, and grant-making skills. Buhl says her knowledge of the nonprofit world and her ability to multitask have been essential to her success on the job. "This is a great job for someone who likes to have a lot of different things to do [though] not so great if you prefer to handle one thing at a time and devote a lot of concentrated quiet time to a task," says Buhl. "This is not a job for a reserved person. The firm's success in pro bono demands that you be an eloquent, enthusiastic, and diplomatic spokesperson for the firm and its pro bono

LAW FIRM PRO BONO COUNSEL: DIFFERENT ENVIRONMENTS

When it comes to pro bono practices, different firms do different things. "My work as Weil Gotshal's pro bono counsel shares many characteristics with similar positions at other firms, while in other respects the jobs vary widely from firm to firm," Buhl explains. "Some directors are partners who carry a fee-generating caseload, others are nonattorneys who manage CSR and public service [or] nonlegal volunteer projects. . . . At the very simplest, our common goal is to develop and maintain the infrastructure that supports a meaningful and sustainable pro bono practice."

work." Networking skills are always important—Buhl says she's even placed projects while riding in the elevator.

"It is also wonderful to be in a position to direct resources to the nonprofits that need them," Buhl states. "Having been in that seat, I know so well the commitment, dedication and professionalism of the nonprofit community, and to help them help others is a tremendous honor and privilege." Buhl recalls one of the first pro bono matters she handled at the firm, a case led by the Innocence Project that resulted in the exoneration of a man who

LAW FIRM PRO BONO COORDINATOR: BREAK-IN TIP

Buhl says that firms seem to be embracing the concept of creating a pro bono director position, and the field is growing. Still, Buhl says pro bono positions at firms are still few and far between and highly coveted. Nonprofit or public interest experience can be a natural stepping-stone into pro bono work at law firms; Buhl had a nonprofit background before joining Weil Gotshal. "I had developed a nice niche in nonprofit management and was very comfortable, although I confess it was starting to become somewhat predictable," she says "My experience as an executive in the nonprofit arena, particularly with volunteer management, as well as my work with attorney volunteers fit well." Another way to get your feet wet is to volunteer to direct pro bono projects at your current law firm—you'll gain valuable experience working with nonprofit organizations and managing attorneys' pro bono work.

91

had been wrongfully imprisoned for seven years. "We were ecstatic," she says. "We've since taken many other equally compelling matters from that organization and, happily, have had similar results."

"This is an endlessly fascinating, challenging, and rewarding job for me because it does draw on so much of my background in the nonprofit area, not [the] least of which is helping people learn something new about their communities and themselves," Buhl explains. "For attorneys who are already tremendously accomplished and bright, this is very special; many times attorneys have told me that pro bono work makes them 'feel like lawyers' again."

Practice Group Manager

Monika Wirtz left a position as a litigation associate at a large law firm just about a year away from being up for partner. "It wasn't what I wanted," she explains. "The cases all became so ginormous. . . . I was managing cases and wasn't doing what I really thought of as lawyering." So Wirtz did a lot of talking with friends and colleagues who had left large firm positions and asked questions about their new jobs; she says she talked with people in many different careers, including in-house counsel, solo practitioners, academics, and one friend who was overseeing a firm's professional development projects. "I thought doing something in firm management would be [a good fit]," Wirtz says. "I liked being part of the big firm."

Wirtz's current position is litigation practice group manager and support attorney at Ropes & Gray, LLP, in Boston. "I support two litigation practice groups," she says, the firm's complex business and securities litigation groups.

Wirtz says her work spans various other departments at the firm, and part of her role is to interface with them. As part of her job, Wirtz keeps track of new decisions and reports that affect her groups, and tracks new cases filed in federal court, looking for preexisting relationships with the parties. She also handles business development—for example, she recently assisted a partner with a pitch to get a specific securities class action, tweaking and redesigning the firm's marketing materials to fit the bill. Wirtz also manages the practice groups' strategic plan, overseeing growth, lateral recruitment, and profitability, and handling lots of "business intelligence research" to help the firm position itself in a way that sets it apart from the competition.

"My job is incredibly varied," Wirtz says, adding that she particularly enjoys strategic planning and positioning projects. "I like the business

92

part of it," she says, "intellectually, [figuring out] how we're going to position ourselves."

PRACTICE GROUP MANAGER: A NOTE ON WORK-LIFE BALANCE

Leaving a practicing position just about a year away from becoming partner couldn't be an easy choice—and Wirtz says many people, including lawyers at her old firm, questioned her decision to leave. But Wirtz says she's received a trade-off: She now has better work-life balance and still plenty of autonomy in her position. Many of the people who are profiled in this book chose to leave private practice for other legal and nonlegal positions (in fact, this book could have been called Leaving Litigation). Law office management is a great fit for those with a JD who understand the legal environment and how lawyers work—like many other nonpracticing JDs, Wirtz says that being an attorney often gets her credibility with her partners.

As with many other law positions in law office management, practice group directors or leaders' job duties and roles may vary by firm. "While we all do the same type of tasks, there may be different emphasis" on some duties over others, Wirtz stresses, depending on the firm. Management skills are integral in practice group leadership, as is the ability to deal with different personality types. "In order to be successful in this position, you have to be able to motivate a lot of different types of people," Wirtz says. That includes "being able to manage up . . . and manage people whom you report to," she adds. Wirtz explains that the role of practice group managers is to stay on top of everyone in the group, partners included. In fact, Wirtz says she gives her partners "homework."

PRACTICE GROUP MANAGER: BREAK-IN TIP

Some JDs can get started in a lower position, such as a practice group coordinator, says Wirtz. She believes a legal background and solid understanding of the practice and business of law are just as important than a business or marketing background, which can be learned through experience.

93

The position's greatest challenge is balancing, which Wirtz says isn't all that different from being an associate. "I'm still the same type-A personality type as I was when I practiced at a large law firm," she says. As a practice group manager, however, Wirtz says she's in the background more. "You can't have a big ego," she says. "To do practice group management, you have to be OK with not being at the forefront."

THERE'S MORE ON THE WEB!
Career Resources for This Chapter

Association of Legal Administrators, http://www.alanet.org/default.aspx
Legal Marketing Association, http://www.legalmarketing.org/
Law Firm Media Professionals, http://www.lfmp.org/
Legal Management Resource Center, run by the ALA, http://thesource.alanet.org/portal/server.pt
ABA Law Practice Management Section, http://www.abanet.org/lpm/home.shtml
National Association of Pro Bono Professionals, http://www.abanet.org/legalservices/probono/napbpro/home.html
Legal Management, trade journal published by ALA, http://www.alanet.org/publications/legalmgmt.aspx
Strategies: The Journal of Legal Marketing, published by LMA, http://www.legalmarketing.org/about-lma/products-and-services/strategies-the-journal-of-legal-marketing/index_html

---

CHAPTER 6

Growing Business and Corporate Careers

According to NALP data, about 14.2 percent of 2006 law graduates chose business or industry positions. Because corporate law departments don't have the same means of training new law graduates as most law firms do, in-house counsel positions may be a better fit for those with previous legal experience who may be looking for a career change. In fact, according to the Association of Corporate Counsel's 2006 Census of In-house Counsel, corporate counsel who responded to the census had worked in other legal positions for an average of six years before going in-house, holding on average of two legal positions beforehand.

One thing is for sure: Corporate work can present plenty of opportunities for able JDs. The Association of Corporate Counsel's website reports that the association represents more than twenty thousand members and over ten thousand organizations. In addition to in-house work, attorneys serve the needs of business and corporate clients as outside counsel at law firms and in other capacities.

Read on for in-house attorneys' and others' experiences in several corporate subspecialties.

Corporate Compliance and Ethics

According to Joe E. Murphy, compliance careers are growing and in great demand. Murphy should know: The self-professed "dean of compliance" wrote the book on compliance careers, *Building a Career in Compliance and*

Ethics (coauthor with Joshua Leet, Society of Corporate Compliance and Ethics, 2007); cofounded Integrity Interactive, an online compliance firm; is a partner in Compliance Systems Legal Group; sits on the board of the Society of Corporate Compliance and Ethics; and edits a journal that addresses issues in corporate ethics and compliance.

Before becoming a compliance practitioner, Murphy spent twenty years working as in-house counsel at Bell Atlantic, where he was involved with antitrust work and corporate compliance. "I realized you had to view the corporation as responsible for every single thing that [every employee does] every single day," he says. "The mission was to make sure that the company did the right thing."

Enter compliance and ethics professionals. "The best [description] of the role of the compliance and ethics person is . . . [that we] use our best

---

CORPORATE COMPLIANCE AND ETHICS: SOME SUBSPECIALTIES

In their book *Building a Career in Compliance and Ethics*, Joe Murphy and Joshua Leet list the following specialties, among many others:

- Chief compliance officer
- Ethics officer
- Business unit compliance officer
- Internal audit
- Security
- Human resources
- Inspector general
- Risk management
- Ombuds
- Privacy officers
- Governance officer
- Sarbanes-Oxley compliance manager
- Corporate responsibility officer
- Regulatory affairs
- Government contracting specialists
- Outside ethics/compliance lawyer or consultant
- Compliance analyst
- Outside investigation firm lawyer
- Background check firm lawyer
- Monitor

---

efforts to prevent and detect misconduct," Murphy says. He describes the job as "going out and looking for trouble" and finding it before it happens, and says ethics positions require multidisciplinary skills. "If you're a compliance person, you've got to convince [perhaps] eighty thousand people to follow every single law every single day," Murphy points out.

Murphy says it's best when one senior officer oversees the company's compliance program, is "responsible for making sure that the compliance and ethics program is implemented and meets the standard and actually works," and has a reporting relationship to the board or upper management. Murphy says each business unit should have people entrusted with compliance responsibilities; in addition, there may be "subject matter experts" who oversee one subset of compliance and ethics issues, such as human resources, internal audit, security, or legal.

Though not all compliance positions require a law degree, "it's very useful to have an understanding of the law and legal system," Murphy says, so a JD is an ideal match for corporate ethics positions. Still, "man agement skills are far more important," says Murphy. He cites communication skills, investigating and auditing skills, and leadership skills as

CORPORATE COMPLIANCE AND ETHICS: BREAK-IN TIP

There aren't many formal educational program options in corporate compliance and ethics, Murphy points out; one option is the certification program offered by the Society for Corporate Compliance and Ethics. Experience, then, can be instrumental in getting started in the field. Murphy says many transfer into compliance and ethics from an in-house counsel position, while a government or law enforcement background is also helpful. Not only does enforcement experience give a candidate credibility, but "companies always have to think 'what if something goes wrong and we have to talk to the government?'" Murphy explains. "Who better to talk to the government than somebody with government background?" Informal experience in compliance can be a way in as well. To those at law firms, for example, Murphy recommends starting the firm's own compliance program—"once you get kicked in the teeth," he says, you will better understand what's involved in the field.

crucial components of the position—for instance, Murphy says public speaking skills can be instrumental in getting people to follow corporate compliance rules.

Murphy describes compliance positions as encompassing three jobs: those of counselor, manager, and cop. "One challenge is getting people to understand what it is you do, what you are," says Murphy. Another is getting them to do the right thing. "You need to be a persistent person," Murphy says. "You may be the only person not being a team player."

In particular, there may be a challenge in "policing up," Murphy says, sometimes having to go against one's boss.

Corporate compliance and ethics careers are "an opportunity to do good and do well at the same time," Murphy believes. "If you can prevent someone from breaking the law, you can save their career, you can save their family. You're really focused on getting people to do the right thing in the business context."

General Counsel

General counsel positions can be as varied as law departments themselves. At large, multinational corporations, general counsel may serve in a C-level management role, overseeing large law departments whose attorneys might specialize in various subsets of corporate law. At small or solo law departments, on the other hand, the general counsel may be a jack-of-all-trades who manages every legal matter that crosses the company's path, from contracts to deals to litigation.

S. Alexander Erlam is of the latter variety: He has founded two law departments at small companies and served as their general counsel. Currently at Vertical Screen, Inc., in Marlton, New Jersey, Erlam says he loves the diversity in his work and the constant opportunity to forge ahead. "I'm not pigeon-holed," he explains. "I love the fact that I can do so many different things." Erlam says he also enjoys working in an in-house environment "where I have one client and represent the corporate identity and interests." Though he focuses quite a bit on privacy law and related issues, Erlam handles everything from negotiating deals to drafting agreements to creating policies and guidelines for the company's clients and vendors.

Erlam recommends that those interested in corporate positions work at a law firm and specialize. He says his specialization in privacy issues has made him more marketable—in fact, he was called by a headhunter for his current position when he wasn't actively seeking work. "You have to be watchful of the market," he warns. "If you're going to find a niche, make sure there's a market for it . . . and it's not too narrow."

GENERAL COUNSEL: DIFFERENT WORK ENVIRONMENTS

At large companies, general counsel typically oversee in-house lawyers in the company's law department, serving in an executive or C-level role. At small or solo law departments, general counsel may be charged with any legal task that the company needs done.

At nonprofit organizations, general counsel may even take on some nonlegal roles and tasks. (See, for example, Chapter 2, which includes insight from Susan Hackett, general counsel at the Association of Corporate Counsel).

Corporate counsel must be "extra organized, extra efficient, [and] knowledgeable about technology," Erlam says. "You have to use every tool you have to get the job done." Being personable is also key. "You need a good personality," Erlam says, adding that corporate attorneys have to get along with their nonattorney managers and colleagues at the company.

And don't buy into the myth that corporate counsel necessarily work less and enjoy better balance, says Erlam. Particularly in small law departments, "the balance is very difficult to get as opposed to a large company where you have help," Erlam says. After all, if you're the only lawyer to handle a deal, you'll be in the office until the deal is complete.

"In-house, it's about getting the job done," Erlam says. "If you work at a law firm and you have a client, that client is passionate about that case." As Erlam says, "If you're working in-house, the client is passionate about pretty much anything you do." The challenge for general counsel—and corporate counsel in general—is often in figuring out how best to further the business of their companies while "working within the confines of the law."

GENERAL COUNSEL: BREAK-IN TIP

Don't be afraid to sell the idea of becoming corporate counsel, Erlam says: He's met general counsel who have pitched the idea of opening up a law department at a company that didn't previously have one. By showing management the benefits of having in-house counsel, savvy attorneys with the right set of skills and experience can create a brand new position—and department. Erlam says he has enjoyed the challenge of organizing and building a law department from the ground up.

Erlam stresses the importance of joining professional organizations, particularly for general counsel at small or solo law departments who don't have the option of turning to a fellow lawyer down the hall with questions. Erlam is active in the Delaware Valley Chapter of the Association of Corporate Counsel and says that his involvement has provided great opportunities for professional development and networking, and also serves as an "extension of his law department."

Corporate counsel positions require hard work, just as much as law firm positions do. "You do a lot in a day," Erlam says. "In my company, if I don't bless an agreement, the deal doesn't happen."

Contracts Attorney

Contract work may be a task that's at the top of most corporate attorneys' lists, but some in-house counsel—particularly at larger law departments—specialize in contracts specifically.

Don C. Brown is a great example—as corporate counsel at DuPont Company in Wilmington, Delaware, Brown negotiates and drafts contracts with the company's suppliers, with a primary focus on raw materials and chemicals.

Brown says he'd always worked primarily in transactional in-house settings. He started out working for the local county and state attorney general's offices, then moved into corporate roles in health care and financial services "where the product of my client was their professional skills," he says. Now at DuPont, Brown represents his client in providing goods and manufacturing services—not a huge step away, he says, but still a different skill.

CONTRACT ATTORNEY: SOME WORK ENVIRONMENTS

Here is just a sampling of the industries that hire corporate counsel to draft and negotiate their contracts in-house:

- Medical
- Pharmaceutical
- Telecommunications
- Software and computers
- Engineering
- Manufacturing
- Insurance
- Transportation
- Federal, state, and municipal government

The key to success in contract work is "being comfortable that you've anticipated the most likely risks and you've drafted to handle them," Brown explains. It's also about problem-solving and solution-finding, he says, and sometimes asking uncomfortable questions to account for the "what ifs." Becoming a good drafter entails "chewing on the idea," says Brown, and anticipating a wide range of problems. Brown brings up a clause accounting for an increase in the price of gas as an example—to whom should the price increase be passed on, and to what extent?

"In order to be effective and valued as an in-house practitioner, you have to have some experience and knowledge in profit/loss, the hard issues of business," says Brown. He adds that litigation experience is also helpful. "You become very good if you've been burned in the past," he says, such as learning from a predecessor's mistakes or a nasty past dispute over a draft. Contract counsel have to be reasonable when negotiating, Brown adds, and be great corporate politicians when dealing with clients and other parties alike.

Finding the right fit isn't a one-sided mission, says Brown. He stresses the importance of making sure that the company shares one's values before going in-house. Brown says the company's culture and messages come across through its corporate attorneys' conduct, whether it be through the language of its contracts or the responsiveness of its attorneys. "The reputation has to be for fairness and honesty," Brown says.

CONTRACT ATTORNEY: BREAK-IN TIP

If you want to work in-house, forget skills alone, says Brown, and think fit. Though skills are important, "many people are skillful," Brown points out. So who among the skillful gets the job? The person who's familiar, has a good reputation and relationship with the law department, and is considered the right fit for the department's culture and environment. Brown says those interested in in-house work need to create enough opportunities to meet with corporate counsel and develop relationships. In addition to networking at professional associations, Brown recommends calling corporate counsel for "networking meetings" and asking them to share what they do on a daily basis in their positions.

Corporate Real Estate Careers

Scott Carter got his start in-house the same way that many other corporate attorneys do: by proving himself as outside counsel. "After law school, I worked for a large national firm doing real estate syndication work," Carter says. "I was exposed to a lot of real estate, but also a lot of tax and corporate work." After six years at the firm, Carter was tapped to go in-house as general counsel of Franklin Street Properties Corp. in Wakefield, Massachusetts. "I did some work for my current employer, although not a lot, and the opportunity came for me to come in-house," Carter explains. "The company never had in-house counsel, so it was a really interesting opportunity to come on board and build the department."

Carter's company is a publicly traded real estate investment trust, which buys, sells, and leases properties across the country. With that comes plenty of real estate work, including drafting and negotiating purchase and sale agreements, lease documents, service contracts, and acquisitions paperwork. But like many corporate counsel who serve small or one-man corporate law departments, Carter's work doesn't just stop at real estate: He also handles SEC and compliance issues, quarterly reporting and filings, corporate contracts, and corporate governance work.

"In some regards, you become more of a general practitioner," says Carter, which is "both the challenging and exciting part. . . . It's challenging because you're constantly going back and having to research things." Still, Carter says he enjoys the diversity of his practice, as well as being privy to the big picture when it comes to the company's operations. "You really have a front row seat into the business and understand how the legal things that you do fit into the business," he says, adding that one of the reasons he was interested in corporate work was his undergraduate background in business and finance. "I always yearned to have exposure to the business side," Carter says. "As outside counsel, I was given a very distinct task that fit into the business model, but I wasn't privy to that bigger business model."

As corporate counsel, "you have to be a good listener [and have] a willingness to understand how the legal work fits into the bigger business context," says Carter. "It's probably not possible to be an expert in every area of law that impacts the company you work for," he adds, but it's essential to be an "expert in areas that affect the company most often," as well as be able to research and call on other experts when needed.

REAL ESTATE: BREAK-IN TIP

Those interested in corporate work at small law departments should expect to be involved in all aspects of the company's legal work, Carter says. He recommends that they start at a firm where they have the opportunity to get to know corporate clients and work closely with them—like Carter, many lawyers get hired by corporate clients after serving the client well as outside counsel.

Carter warns against the misperception that corporate work always entails shorter hours and less work than working for a law firm. "Like anything, that just depends on what's going on [at the company]," he says; it can also be affected by the company's size, management, and corporate environment.

Being in-house "is a very exciting way to practice law," Carter believes. "You have the opportunity to be exposed to new things all the time."

Licensing/In-house Intellectual Property Attorney

Intellectual property has ramifications for the whole company, says Douglas Luftman, associate general counsel of intellectual property (IP) at Palm, Inc., in Sunnyvale, California, so IP in-house counsel play an integral role not only in maintaining the company's IP portfolio, but also

103

the big picture: managing the way intellectual property fits into the company's business overall.

Luftman oversees overall IP strategy for Palm, including the company's patents, trade secrets, and copyrights strategy. "I understand all the market differentiations in our products and make sure that we protect them," Luftman says. Luftman graduated law school during the high-tech boom and started at Fenwick & West, a law firm that he describes as forward thinking. When a small start-up client approached him, Luftman went in-house as the company's general counsel; he then worked for a variety of corporate law departments, ranging in size from small to large, including Intel. "I caught the in-house bug," he says. "I wanted to have a cradle-to-grave [understanding] as to how I saw the results of my labor . . . and get to see all the different facets of the business."

LICENSING/IN-HOUSE INTELLECTUAL PROPERTY ATTORNEY: SOME SUBSPECIALTIES OR TASKS

- IP strategy
- Trade secret management
- Patent prosecution
- Patent licensing
- Technology/open source licensing
- Patent searches
- Government affairs
- IP litigation
- Copyrights
- Trademarks
- International IP

One of the greatest challenges of in-house IP work is in resources, says Luftman. "At law firms, there's no real restriction on resources because you're being billed out at an hourly rate," he explains; in-house, the billable hour is taken away and resources and time need to be allocated according to the company's business needs and interests. In-house counsel have to be aware of risks and able to allocate risk, Luftman says. "When you're in-house, you're no longer the top dog," he says. "You're viewed as a cost center."

Analytical and project management skills are also important, he says. Luftman explains that in-house counsel need to "see above the trees [to] the forest" and understand the most important issues about the company's intellectual property and business in general.

LICENSING/IN-HOUSE INTELLECTUAL PROPERTY ATTORNEY: BREAK-IN TIP

As in any other intellectual property position, Luftman says, a technical degree is important, even if an attorney isn't practicing in front of the U.S. PTO. Not only does a technical degree help in-house IP counsel better understand the terminology and technical issues, but Luftman says his engineering degree also taught him to be methodical and get used to a large work load.

Luftman describes his work as "organic IP strategy," which runs across the board, and says the company's appreciation of its intellectual property plays a big part in his success on the job. It's essential "to go to an organization that values intellectual property and views it as a business tool," he explains.

Mergers and Acquisitions Careers

Overseeing mergers and acquisitions work at Tessera, Inc., a technology company in San Jose, California, Taraneh Maghame handles negotiations; drafts documents such as licenses, acquisition agreements, and letters of intent; oversees outside counsel; manages due diligence; and performs extensive document review. "We're always looking for good, fitting technologies that we can acquire," says Maghame, who serves as the company's VP and counsel for mergers and acquisitions and government relations. "My role is to give them all of the legal support [they need] for that." After a deal is done, Maghame stays involved in the integration process and helps ensure that there's a smooth handoff.

Maghame came into her current role from an intellectual property background. She worked in litigation for ten years, handling mostly IP matters at law firms, and then was recruited by Compaq to go in-house and manage the computer company's IP litigation. When the company was acquired by Hewlett Packard, Maghame continued to handle IP litigation matters, as well as licensing and mergers and acquisitions support work. She was then hired by her current company to support its emerging markets and technologies group. Maghame supports all of the mergers and acquisitions activity, and also helps with litigation support

105

work, lobbying, and government relations. Many of the deals she works on are international, she says.

In mergers and acquisitions, "you need to have good business sense," Maghame says. "The business judgment aspect of it is much more critical." In your role as in-house counsel, she says, management may "look more to you to weigh the pros and cons and then guide them to the right decision." Maghame also stresses the importance of prioritizing and organizational skills. "There's a lot going on at the same time" during mergers and acquisitions, she says. Unlike litigation, where the client's case follows one track, mergers and acquisitions tend to have many different tracks—from evaluating IP portfolios to complying with due diligence to drafting documents. Plus, mergers and acquisitions lawyers—and corporate lawyers in general—need to have strong management skills, as they are often in charge of outside counsel.

MERGERS AND ACQUISITIONS CAREERS: BREAK-IN TIP

Maghame recommends that attorneys interested in mergers and acquisitions work get exposed to business. She also says that a broad substantive base is necessary. "It's beneficial to have a more well-rounded experience before you go in-house," Maghame says. "It's not just a matter of the [corporate] documents: You need to assess the risks associated with ongoing litigation and evaluate [the other company's] IP portfolio," among many other tasks. "It's good to have that broad experience," she says. But she says it's better to focus on fields that deal with corporate law—such as corporate contracts—than those that don't.

Though it can be challenging to juggle all of the different tasks associated with mergers and acquisitions, the field can also make for a fast-paced, exciting work environment. For Maghame, the most fulfilling part of the job is "the interesting work that we do [and] the diversity and high-caliber of the people I work with," she says.

Finance and Banking Career Options

When Wall Street began cutting jobs a few years ago, Nikon Limberis decided to go to law school. As an assistant working at the equity trading desk of a large investment banking company at the time, Limberis figured a law degree would offer him versatility, better credentials, and the opportunity for a backup career plan in case his banking options didn't work out. Enrolled in part-time evening classes, Limberis would go to school directly from his job at the trading desk. The most challenging part? Shifting his way of thinking, Limberis says, from that of a banker to that of an attorney—sometimes having to get into "law school mindset" quickly on the subway.

But Limberis was no stranger to challenges. By this time, he had helped build up his current investment company's new offices from scratch, after the company's original offices were lost in the attacks on September 11. Limberis had been hired just before the attacks, and the company called him months later to see if he was still interested in working for them. Limberis started part-time initially and then moved into a full-time position.

Now an associate director at Sandler O'Neill & Partners in Manhattan, Limberis meets daily with research analysts, takes trade orders from clients, and fulfills them. After graduating law school in 2007, Limberis stayed in banking; he says he sees many investment bankers with JD degrees, which offer more versatility and better analytical skills than master's degrees.

"[The JD] has given me confidence," Limberis says. "People react to you differently; when I listen to a research analyst, I am constantly thinking about the other side of the argument." The JD is also helpful when "looking at corporate entities and structures," Limberis says, adding he is often called to explain legal terms and issues at meetings, such as the time he talked about class action suits against companies covered by his employer, or when he explained injunctions in the case of a bank which was being acquired by another entity.

FINANCE AND BANKING CAREER OPTIONS: BREAK-IN TIP

Because the skill set required of a banker differs from that of a lawyer, Limberis recommends having some financial background or experience before applying for banking positions—an internship with an investment firm, for instance. He also says that there are some legal courses that are particularly helpful, such as corporate law, banking law, and international law. Though financial and math knowledge is important, Limberis points out that banking is more than just being able to read balance sheets: It's about building relationships and requires strong people skills.

Like many other alternative careers, banking offers better work-life balance than law practice, Limberis believes—though he says he put in long days when he first started in his field. He also cites his salary and bonuses as perks for using his legal education in the field of finances, and says that for him, going to a law firm would mean taking a pay cut. Still, Limberis eventually hopes to use his law degree not only on his current job, but also in practice, such as giving pro bono advice to those who need it or even transitioning into a corporate counsel position.

THERE'S MORE ON THE WEB!
Career Resources for This Chapter

Association of Corporate Counsel, http://www.acc.com/
ABA Section of Business Law, http://www.abanet.org/buslaw/home.shtml
The Society of Corporate Compliance and Ethics, http://www.corporatecompliance.org//AM/Template.cfm?Section=Home
Minority Corporate Counsel Association, http://www.mcca.com/
Business Law Today, published by the ABA Section of Business Law, http://www.abanet.org/buslaw/blt/
Business Lawyer, quarterly trade journal published by the ABA Section of Business Law, http://www.abanet.org/buslaw/tbl/home.shtml
ACC Docket, published by ACC, http://www.acc.com/php/cms/index.php?id=38
American Bankers Association, http://www.aba.com/
National Investment Banking Association, http://www.nibanet.org/
Finance Leaders Association, http://www.financeleaders.org/

CHAPTER 7

Self-Employment Options

Law firms need help—services from skilled and capable professionals, that is, in every imaginable arena from staffing to writing to marketing. And often that help comes from self-employed JDs, business owners who have carved out a niche for themselves by providing a specific legal service to other attorneys and law firms. In addition, self-employed sole practitioners and general practitioners provide legal services to the public.

This chapter describes several opportunities for self-employment. JDs tell their stories of founding their own businesses or becoming self-employed, sharing valuable tips and advice for striking out on your own. Their businesses run the gamut, but the owners share some common characteristics: drive, passion, and the ability to pinpoint and capitalize on their own strengths and talents.

Note that while you can start virtually any business with a law degree, these are legal-oriented businesses. They focus on sole practitioner opportunities, as well as services provided to law firms, attorneys, and other legal employers—so if you're looking for help with your long-sought goal of opening a bakery, this chapter isn't your best bet. But if you're thinking about becoming self-employed and offering a legal-oriented service, read on for others' experiences.

Solo Practitioners and Small Law Firm Owners

Let's start with the obvious: Many attorneys make a great career out of practicing on their own or founding their own small law firms.

When Jennifer Ator left her large firm to start her own small firm, she says she went through culture shock: All of the minutiae she used to have

---

SOLO PRACTICE: SOME PRACTICE AREAS

On what areas do solo practitioners concentrate? Anything, really. The ABA General Practice, Solo, and Small Firm Division lists the following practice area committees on its website:

- Business Law Group
- Agricultural
- Bankruptcy
- Business, Business Opportunities, and Commercial Law
- Gaming Law
- Intellectual Property Law
- International Law
- Urban, State, and Local Law
- Estate and Financial Planning Group
- Business Advice and Financial Planning
- Estate Planning, Probate, and Trust
- Taxation
- Family Law Group
- Elder Law
- Family Law
- Juvenile Law
- Litigation Group
- Alternative Dispute Resolution
- Criminal Law
- Immigration Law
- Labor, Employment, and Civil Rights Law
- Litigation
- Tort and Insurance Practice
- Workers Compensation
- Real Estate Law Group
- Construction Law
- Environmental, Natural Resources, and Energy Law
- Real Estate Law

---

assistance with now had to be done by her, from addressing envelopes to dealing with accounting. She first went into business with two other attorneys, each one handling his or her own specialty; then she set out on her own; and then finally merged her practice with another sole practitioner to form Hankins & Ator. Practicing in Miami Springs, Florida, and connecting with her partner—who's at another location—online, Ator focuses on employment law and commercial litigation.

Jeff Allen started his firm twelve years ago, after practicing in a partnership for years; at Graves & Allen in Oakland, California, he has a general civil practice with an emphasis on real estate and business matters. "You've got to be a self-starter," says Allen about opening a law practice. "There's not going to be a partner on top of you" to encourage getting the work done. Allen and Ator also say that solo practitioners must be personable in order to convince the client to come through the door. Being able to set up a network is essential, Ator says. "You have to know people," she says, as solo and small firm practice is a referral-based business. "In my experience, that's the best way to practice."

For Ator, the biggest challenge of running a small firm is the business aspect: keeping up with accounting, payroll, filing, and other business paperwork. "One of the huge mistakes that everyone makes is [thinking] 'I'm going to do this all myself,'" she says. "It keeps you from being able to develop your own business." Ator notes that it's essential to find people who can be trusted to handle the business side of a solo or small firm's business, like accounting and technology.

SOLO PRACTICE: BREAK-IN TIP

Allen says lawyers should have experience practicing law before they strike out on their own. "You have to be able to think like a lawyer and act like a lawyer," he says. "Don't become a sole practitioner until you've learned how to practice law." Plus, "at larger firms, you have many attorneys to bounce ideas off of," Allen says. "You don't have that if you're a sole practitioner." Many experienced solos share Allen's sentiment, though it isn't impossible to start out soon after graduation. (See the chapters on elder law, entertainment law, and immigration law for some examples of people who did just that). If you are going to start your own firm right out of law school, Allen says getting a mentor is imperative—join professional associations and committees to meet others who have experience practicing on their own.

Allen notes that he planned for six months before opening his firm, and says he already had experience running a law firm in his prior partnership. "You need to be planning for the ability to stay in business when you don't have a lot of clients at first," he says. Allen adds that sole practitioners must consider all aspects of the business before starting out—available savings or a line of credit, for example; the equipment and space needed; and any employees to hire.

Being self-employed provides plenty of flexibility. "You get to make all the decisions," says Allen. "You get to decide if you want to take a case." Ator agrees: "I like to be able to fire my clients," she says. "I've had clients as a solo . . . who are willing to invest in me to learn their business so that I can essentially be a partner with them."

Legal Research and Writing Careers

Lisa Solomon has always enjoyed research and writing—throughout law school, even college, and while starting her legal career as a litigation associate at a small, boutique Manhattan firm. So when signs indicated that the firm was preparing to close down, Solomon decided to use her best talents to her advantage: She went to work for Lexis-Nexis as a product trainer at area law schools. Solomon was later approached by the law firm where she worked as a paralegal during college—with which she had kept in touch—to handle some of the firm's writing remotely. While doing work for the firm, Solomon also founded and grew her legal research and writing business, providing services to small firms and solo practitioners.

For some attorneys, contract work—whether research and writing, document review, or other projects—can be a great way to supplement a solo practitioner's income. Solomon, however, has relied exclusively on her research and writing firm since 1996, positioning herself as a research and writing attorney, working on a contract basis, and never signing on as counsel of record. "I prefer it that way," she says. "I get to do what I want, and frankly, what I am good at."

Solomon handles a wide variety of writing projects, from appellate briefs to trial motions. She also performs legal and factual research for clients; sometimes, she is hired to edit other attorneys' writing. Because she handles cases in all civil areas, Solomon says she is always learning something new, which makes the work exciting. "It is intellectually stimulating," she says. "I help strategize with the lawyers that I'm working with." And because her clients are attorneys, Solomon says she feels her work is respected and appreciated. "It's rewarding to have clients who really understand what you do and respect what you do," she explains.

Solomon says much of the business's growth can be attributed to technological advances. "When I first started, I had clients who didn't even have email," she says. "These days, people are getting used to the technology that enables a practice like this to grow." Much of the work can be done remotely, through email or fax—in fact, Solomon says she has clients from all over the United States, and even the Virgin Islands, and has not met the majority of them! The ability to do the work pretty much anytime and anyplace also makes for a much more flexible environment, Solomon says, which can provide better work-life balance and alternative schedule arrangements. Plus, because much of the work can be done from a small office, or even a home office, overhead tends to be pretty low.

LEGAL RESEARCH AND WRITING CAREERS: BREAK-IN TIP

As with any other business, getting started can be the toughest part in legal research and writing. One great thing with this particular service? The "tools of the trade" are simple, and most JDs probably already have them, Solomon points out in an article she wrote for *GP/Solo Magazine*, a publication of the ABA Section of General and Solo Practice. Generally, a computer, phone, high-speed Internet access, and subscription to a comprehensive legal research database service are all that's needed to get started, Solomon says. And because legal researchers and writers serve attorneys, getting clients often starts with networking at professional and trade association events. Research and writing attorneys—like any self-employed people—have to worry about business issues and concerns, including marketing and planning. "You have to be self-motivated; you have to have a degree of self-confidence," says Solomon. "You have to feel comfortable with not having a paycheck every two weeks."

Solomon says there is a huge unmet demand when it comes to legal research and writing services, particularly at small firms and sole practitioners. "Solos get overwhelmed, too, and they don't have the employees to pass work down to," she says. In addition, Solomon says some lawyers simply don't like research and writing, or are not very good at them. Outsourcing research and writing tasks can prove profitable, as in most states, the hiring attorney can not only recover from the client for the writing attorney's time, but also make a profit on it. "It's all the benefits of having an associate without all of the 'negatives,'" says Solomon, such as overhead costs, taxes, and long-term commitments. "Not everybody who has a temporary crunch wants to hire someone full time."

Plus, Solomon says opportunities for expansion aren't just in the legal field. "Being a good writer and a persuasive writer is transferable," she believes. "You can expand your horizons." For example, Solomon also handles some public relations and even writes and designs greeting cards and other humorous gifts for attorneys.

Legal writing in the strictest sense—think memos, motions, and briefs—isn't the only avenue where JDs can turn their writing skills into lucrative employment. Legal publishers, trade publications, and even nonlegal magazines and newspapers hire JDs to write articles, stories, news briefs, and books relating to the law.

When Meg Charendoff became pregnant with twins, she quit her job as a litigation associate and eventually turned to freelance writing as her new career, publishing articles and even creative nonfiction chapters in the popular Chicken Soup for the Soul series of books. She pitched a story to an editor at the *Pennsylvania Law Weekly*, a publication of American Law Media (ALM), who approached Charendoff about becoming a staff writer. By the time she came in for her interview with the editor in chief, the company needed her in another role: She was offered the chance to become the editor of ALM's magazines.

As an editor, Charendoff plans editorial calendars for her publications, consults with freelance writers on topics, assigns articles, edits articles as they come in, and works with her production team to get the magazines out to press. She works on a weekly newspaper, a quarterly trade publication for corporate counsel, and ALM's annual "State of the Profession" project.

Besides enjoying her work with a great staff and freelancers, Charendoff says she enjoys the flexibility her job affords. "I have a great deal of flexibility when it comes to my kids," says Charendoff. She also says she gets to meet many interesting people—after all, a writer's job is to talk to different people daily to get the story.

Charendoff says the JD degree is helpful in her position. "When I work on the newspapers, an understanding of the law can be helpful," she says. Plus, "having JD after my name often opens doors" that might otherwise be closed, she says, especially when talking with other lawyers, partners, or higher-ups at companies and firms.

"In some respects, a lot of any job is not what you know, but how you marshal your resources to learn what you need to know," Charendoff says. "It's knowing where to look; it's knowing whom to turn to when you need help." Though she didn't have editorial experience when she started at ALM, Charendoff had resources, contacts, and experience as a freelance writer, which helped her land the job. "You can learn your craft, but you've got to have some intuition for it," she says. "Know what you want to do, and the 'how' will take care of itself."

LEGAL RESEARCH AND WRITING CAREERS: SOME EMPLOYERS OR CLIENTS

Self-employment: providing research and writing services to other attorneys and law firms

- Legal research and writing firms
- Legal publishers
- Legal trade publications
- Nonlegal publishers and publications looking for legal expertise
- Law firms looking for in-house writers

Legal Staffing Business Owner

After building the law department of a newly created leasing subsidiary at a top national life insurance company, Robert Murphy was no stranger to being a trailblazer and entrepreneur. Murphy worked as in-house counsel from the late 1970s to 1991, serving in various capacities from investment real estate attorney to general counsel. When his company was sold in 1991, Murphy decided to become self-employed. "I wanted to chart a new course," he explains. "I was not enthused about practicing law and wanted to try my hand in business."

After first founding a brokerage company, Murphy saw a potential in legal staffing. At the time, "we thought there might be opportunity, [but] we didn't know if there would be need," he says. Today, Murphy says the legal staffing industry enjoys a twenty-year track record; at this point, the focus has shifted to what each company can offer to the field. His business, Assigned Counsel, Inc., headquartered in Wayne, Pennsylvania, provides temporary attorneys to law firms, corporate law departments, and other employers.

Gregg Schor also went into business for himself when his former employer, a venture-capital company, was acquired by a larger company—formerly general counsel of the smaller firm, Schor was laid off. Though he planned to take some time off, Schor didn't get much chance to relax: Some of the people he'd worked with in the past at other corporate law departments began calling on him for temporary help with poorly written contracts and deal negotiations. Essentially, his new clients relied on Schor to act as their part-time general counsel—working remotely

115

and on his own terms, but providing continuous help with the law department's needs.

Schor recognized an unmet need and founded General Counsel Solutions in New York City, which provides part-time general counsel services to corporate law departments. Today, Schor has a staff of attorneys, but the idea is still the same as when he first started contract work: to provide ongoing and continuous legal services that a company can rely on. Rather than offering a temporary attorney who's called in when the company needs extra legal help, Schor offers an attorney who takes the place of the general counsel—or even the law department—at smaller companies who can't afford or don't need full-time legal employees.

Murphy says his JD degree helps him not just in conversations and dealings with lawyers but also in business-oriented thinking. "The mental training of analyzing situations is the best skill orientation a person in business could have," believes Murphy. Schor says the JD gives a certain confidence level and great research skills: Even if you don't know something [about a particular topic], a legal education has probably taught you where and how to [conduct] research.

Yet while lawyers are trained to think of the legal implications of every decision they make, those who are in business must think first of business implications, Murphy adds. "Any lawyer wanting to go into business would be very well served having support skills in two areas: negotiations . . . and business for lawyers," Murphy says. The first skill, he explains, involves understanding how to make deals and win for both sides, as well as knowing "when it's time to fold and walk"; the second involves business and financial skills not taught in law school, such as reading a balance sheet.

"As a small business owner, the day can have any number of challenges totally unrelated to the law, from finance issues to personnel issues to strategic management," Murphy says. "The fun of the business is also the challenge of the business in that no day can be typecast in the beginning." And as with any other business, a legal business can mean risk—for starters, not knowing where your next paycheck will come from, says Schor. Still, "when the check comes, it's all yours," Schor says. "Plus, you make all the decisions; you allocate your time [as you wish]."

Before getting started in business, Schor recommends that JDs get experience in an area of law that will interest them. Schor knows all about participating in different experiences: He handled all kinds of deals and negotiations, from opening up European subsidiaries at a software company to preserving a company's intellectual property rights during the dissolution of a joint venture. "It's the experience that matters," he says. "Also, you can't put a price on networking and connections."

LEGAL STAFFING BUSINESS OWNER: BREAK-IN TIP

Murphy concedes that it's difficult to get started in business, particularly right out of law school (in fact, he says it's difficult to get into anything but the practice of law right after graduation). Murphy says that while some attorneys go into business for themselves after making a conscious choice, others are pushed into it through circumstances—such as losing a job or needing better work-life balance. "The key, if you're going to go into business, is to recognize that you're going to have to demonstrate flexibility," Murphy says. Business is not a predictable activity, he says, adding that it took him thirteen months to get his first client once he started his business. "It's [about] having flexibility and staying power," says Murphy, "recognizing that six months down the road, you may have to change your business model."

Legal business owners and service providers must be prepared to go that extra mile for clients. "You have to have great work ethic; you have to have great people skills," Schor says. "People have to want to give you [their] business."

Legal Service Providers

Want to open up a business that serves attorneys and the legal field? You have plenty of options. Here are just a few services to consider:

- Legal staffing: providing temporary or long-term attorneys and legal staff to law firms and other legal employers (see subsection on this specialty above)
- Legal recruiting: finding attorney and nonattorney talent for law firms and other legal employers (see subsection on this specialty below)
- Contract attorney services: providing document review, drafting, and other services to law firms and attorneys on a contract or temporary basis
- Service of process and related services
- Litigation support: providing a comprehensive array of litigation support services

117

- Trial or litigation consulting: assisting lawyers with trial strategy, jury selection, and other litigation matters
- Legal research and writing: assisting law firms and attorneys with research projects; writing memos, briefs, and other documents; and providing nonlegal writing services (see subsection on this specialty below)
- Exhibit and graphics preparation: preparing trial graphics, exhibits, "day-in the-life" videos, settlement brochures, and other litigation tools
- Electronic discovery services: managing, maintaining, uploading, and cataloging firms' e-discovery
- Legal marketing or public relations: assisting firms and attorneys with marketing, strategic planning, business development, and public or media relations
- Legal investigation: helping attorneys find the facts through interviews and investigation, product research, and record checking

Though all of these business ideas have differences, they have one thing in common: Your involvement and ownership of them is enhanced by your JD degree. Your legal education provides you with substantive background and an understanding of the legal process and environment, which can give you a leg up over non-JD legal business providers. Plus, many legal business owners say their JDs give them more credibility with their clients: other attorneys and firms.

Of course, it's important to note that you must have the requisite skills and aptitude to perform the specific service you choose to provide—so don't pick litigation support, for example, if you've never seen the inside of a courtroom! To help you determine what might be a good fit, assess your skills, education, and expertise—what do you do well? What niche might you carve out for yourself successfully? Then, figure out if there is a demand for that niche; who your potential clients are; who your competitors are; and what steps you need to take to offer the service you selected on a contract or self-employed basis.

Jim Wagner left a large law firm practice when a client asked him to go in-house and serve as the chief operating officer of a document services business. Though Wagner enjoyed practicing law, he always considered himself an entrepreneurial spirit. "I saw this as an opportunity to go out and develop a new skill set," he says.

"It quickly became apparent that there were a whole other [range of] services that were technology based," Wagner says. In 2005, Wagner cofounded DiscoverReady, a company that manages clients' document review, helps develop discovery strategies, and provides strategic discovery support. He now serves as the company's CEO.

Wagner says his experience practicing law was invaluable in giving him exposure to a range of areas in the legal field, as well as instilling and developing a great work ethic.

To those interested in starting their own legal service business, Wagner says it's essential to have a clear plan and an understanding of their chosen business models. "Look at your model and decide what it is that you really want to accomplish," he says. "Having a great idea does not translate into having a business. You have to be able to sell and execute it."

Communication and people skills are essential for success in self-employment. Wagner also emphasizes the need for start-up capital—even after opening up a business, it takes a while to retain clients and bill and collect for services, he points out. He also notes the need to keep track of conflicts and maintain a thorough conflicts database as top business priorities.

SELF-EMPLOYMENT: BREAK-IN TIP

In thinking about starting the "perfect" business, "don't force it," says Wagner. "If you do, you could invest and decide this is the [business model] you want to go after, and then decide it's not the right one." Instead, invest some initial time and resources in figuring out what niches in the marketplace aren't yet filled. Then, "stick to whatever it is you're doing," Wagner advises. "Every day that I'm working, I'm thinking of how I can do a better job."

Wagner is quick to dispel the myth that a nonpracticing legal career is just about "choosing lifestyle." As a business owner, Wagner says he is constantly on duty, with his clients serving as his bosses now. Still, being self-employed does afford a greater sense of control over one's destiny, he adds. A legal service business can be a meaningful and rewarding alternative career path.

Careers in Alternative Dispute Resolution

Some attorneys find full-time, part-time, or contract work in alternative dispute resolution. Attorney arbitrators and mediators help resolve disputes without going to trial. According to JAMS (Judicial Arbitration and Mediation Services), a national dispute resolution provider that employs many attorneys and judges, arbitration has long been "used as an alternative to litigation in commercial and labor disputes[;] this dispute resolution process offers less formal procedures, abbreviated presentations and the undivided attention of the neutral(s). The arbitrator rules on discovery requests and disputes. The process can be binding or non-binding." A mediator is a "neutral professional who facilitates negotiations between disputing parties and may evaluate the relative merits of the claims and defenses. The mediator does not have power to impose a solution or decision—the parties retain ultimate control over the outcome. He/she sets the ground rules and may profoundly affect the order of the proceedings, the parties' collective and individual analyses, and the general dynamic of the settlement discussion. A mediator can be a private judge, facilitator, special master (or referee), neutral advisor or anyone selected by mutual agreement of the parties to the dispute."

Jeff Allen of Graves & Allen in Oakland (see the solo practitioner section above) serves as a mediator in many different types of disputes, including torts, real estate disputes, construction cases, business disputes, and nonmarital partners' disputes.

ARBITRATION/MEDIATION: SOME AREAS OF PRACTICE

On its website, JAMS includes the following areas in alternative dispute resolution:

- Arbitration practice
- Bankruptcy practice
- Class action and mass torts
- Construction practice
- Employment practice
- Government practice
- International practice

Allen says mediation can be a particularly good fit for sole practitioners, as the process doesn't necessarily require a large office or lots of other peripherals. He says mediators need to be knowledgeable about the subject areas in which they practice, and also have excellent people skills. "You need to be able to maintain equanimity under adverse conditions," he says; to gain people's trust and get them to come out of their shells.

ARBITRATION/MEDIATION: BREAK-IN TIP

Allen recommends getting on a mediation panel, which can be a good way to get referrals. He notes that most panels require training in mediation, including a formal course.

For Allen, the most rewarding part of mediation is "being able to settle a lawsuit," he says. "I am taking people out of a very difficult situation and improving their lives."

Legal Recruiter

There's a simple reason for the growth of career opportunities in legal recruiting. "Great companies and great law firms are always in need of great talent," explains Charles Volkert, executive director of Robert Half Legal. And for those looking to blend a legal education with a business or sales approach, legal recruiting can present a great career option.

Volkert started in recruiting nearly nine years ago, after realizing he didn't want to practice law long term. His wife, an IT recruiter, advised Volkert that Robert Half was looking to open up a legal division; Volkert began as an account executive and managed temporary attorneys and legal staff, then moved into the permanent placement division. Much of the job entails working with people: calling potential candidates and employers, and meeting with law firms and legal departments to share candidates. Yet "a lot of it is pure sales, marketing, outreach, and business development," says Volkert, so sales-minded and business-savvy JDs may fare better in legal recruiting.

Like Volkert, Katie Weiss considered legal recruiting after she grew restless as a litigation associate; her sister worked for Robert Half and suggested that Weiss approach the company's legal recruiting division. Weiss joined the company in 2005, when a new opening was created for her. As an attorney recruiter, Weiss says she spends most of her day on the phone, either cold-calling or "warm-calling" people from her existing database.

A huge part of a recruiter's job is networking, building rapport and trust, and learning about the needs of employer clients, says Volkert. "Any successful legal recruiter really has the passion to get on the phone, get out and meet people, be proactive, and not take 'no' as a rejection," he says.

121

"You have to get people to trust you," agrees Weiss, and be "able to read people well and to have a good conversation on the phone." Following up with clients—even where there is no immediate gain—is also important, says Volkert: He recalls spending time on one attorney's résumé even after it was apparent that he wouldn't be able to place the candidate and says he received tremendous satisfaction when the candidate received several offers on his own and called Volkert to thank him for his help.

Legal recruiters must also know and understand the legal industry and marketplace. Volkert stresses the importance of having formal legal background and says most of his employees come in with legal experience. "[Law school] prepared me for legal recruiting in understanding what exactly attorneys do," says Weiss. She says her law degree helps give her more clout with clients and candidates.

LEGAL RECRUITER: SOME SUBSPECIALTIES

- Lateral hiring
- Junior or new associate hiring
- Partner recruiting
- Legal staff hiring
- Temporary hires
- Contract attorneys and legal staff

Weiss says the best part of the job is getting to meet and talk with many different people on a daily basis—something she says she missed while practicing. Finding a great match and bringing people together is also rewarding, says Volkert, particularly when placing candidates who had been unemployed or unhappy, or when meeting the needs of clients whose goals hadn't been met in the past because they didn't have the right talent.

There's an element of recruiting that requires the ability to be a self-starter. Depending on the positions for which one is recruiting, "the 'sales cycle' can be pretty long," says Weiss. Compensation is usually based on commission, so recruiters have to be able to weather the ups and downs of the legal employment market and "roll with the punches," Weiss says. And because of those ups and downs, finding great talent—particularly for a specialized practice area—can also be difficult. Though recruiting can be a great option for self-employment for JDs with the right skill set and contacts, Weiss says she enjoys having an established firm behind her, particularly in terms of training and support.

LEGAL RECRUITING: BREAK-IN TIP

There is perhaps no other legal job where networking is more important than in legal recruiting. In fact, Weiss says she started her recruiting career by contacting her friends and those she already knew in the field, gradually adding to her list of contacts. "Law school didn't prepare me for networking," says Weiss. She adds that networking should begin as early as law school; she recommends that JDs, new grads, and students join a few different trade organizations and groups that might be beneficial for their careers. She also recommends coming up with a "commercial" or sound byte to capture "who you are and what you bring to the table," Weiss says. "Networking doesn't necessarily mean [meeting] somebody who can get you a job right now," she adds, advising JDs to be open to all relationships.

Attorneys who are seeking to move away from traditional law practice may find an alternative legal career, such as recruiting, to be the right fit. But focusing on the fit is essential, Volkert notes: Don't enter recruiting, for example, as something you might just try out, but rather as a career path you've carefully chosen. "You need to take a long-term view," he says. "You need to find the right home, the right career fit." Legal recruiting is a career choice, Weiss agrees. "It's certainly not for every lawyer who is unhappy and wants to work in an alternative career," she says. "It is a numbers-driven business that can be a lot of pressure; it's really fast paced and you have to make decisions very quickly sometimes."

Volkert recommends shadowing a recruiter, and "if you don't see yourself doing it, you'd better look for a different career," he says. He also recommends that anyone seeking a career change put together a list of "pros and cons" of their ultimate career goals and the job opportunities that might offer ways of reaching those goals. For those interested in legal recruiting, viewing the industry as a never-ending opportunity for growth is important, says Volkert.

Legal Consultant

"Legal consulting is business and management consulting for the legal profession," says Jim Wilber, principal and managing partner at Altman Weil, who works out of the consulting firm's Milwaukee office. Wilber helps firms on strategic issues, such as managing their offers, compensation, and executive searches; at law departments, he also helps with outside counsel management.

Prior to joining Altman Weil, Wilber practiced law at a firm for two and a half years; he worked in legal aid for five years, where he also managed other lawyers; and then he went to a corporate law department for another seven years. His broad experience helps him on the job when dealing with different legal employers and environments, but Wilber says a law degree isn't as important in his position as a background in business and management. "The most important [skill] is the ability to win the confidence of your client and establish a relationship where you are a trusted advisor," Wilber notes.

LEGAL CONSULTING: BREAK-IN TIP

To break in, "you need to emphasize management experience you've had," says Wilber, such as being the head of a practice group or supervising associates. Business management education and experience running things in a law firm or at another legal employer are good skills to bring into a consulting role.

Wilber has built invaluable relationships in the legal profession in his work as a consultant. "As a lawyer, it's gotten me to places in the legal profession I never would have gotten to just by practicing," he says. Wilber says his work allows him to get a broad view of the legal profession and constantly work on fresh, new, exciting projects.

In addition, Wilber says he's gotten to travel extensively—all of his work is on site at client's offices, whether it be across the state or across the pond. The travel can prove challenging: Wilber says on average, he travels three days a week. Recently, for example, he assisted the Supreme Court of Louisiana with assessing the strengths and weaknesses of its lawyer disciplinary system; he also helped legal aid services in North Carolina find alternative funding.

Legal consultants are in demand by busy lawyers who don't want to—or don't have time to—deal with the business of law. It may be a profession, but the law is also big business. As Wilber puts it, "the business of law is subject to the law of business."

THERE'S MORE ON THE WEB!

Career Resources for This Chapter

ABA General Practice, Solo, and Small Firm Division, http://www.abanet.org/genpractice/home.html

ABA Law Practice Management Section, http://www.abanet.org/lpm/home.shtml

The American Society of Legal Writers, http://www.scribes.org/

National Association of Legal Search Consultants, http://www.nalsc.org/

ABA Section of Dispute Resolution, http://www.abanet.org/dispute/home.html

American Arbitration Association, www.adr.org

The Association of Attorney-Mediators, http://www.attorney-mediators.org/links.cfm

JAMS, http://www.endispute.com/

Litigation Support Vendors Association, http://lsva.com/pn/

GPSolo Magazine, published by the ABA General Practice, Solo, and Small Firm Division, http://www.abanet.org/genpractice/magazine/index.html

National Association of Legal Search Consultants, http://www.nalsc.org/

CHAPTER 8

Tips from Career Services Professionals

Whether you're a law student, new graduate, or seasoned lawyer looking to make a career change, you can take advantage of the services offered by your law school's career services professionals. They can be invaluable in many ways to students and alumni grappling with career decisions: pinpointing career options, offering help with résumés, referring candidates to job openings and networking opportunities, and introducing you to career resources and materials. They can be invaluable in many ways to students and alumni grappling with career decisions: pinpointing career options, offering help with résumés, referring candidates to job openings and networking opportunities, and introducing you to career resources and materials. They can be invaluable in many ways to students and alumni grappling with career decisions.

In this chapter, career services professionals share tips for finding the career that is the right fit for you.

If you're just getting started . . .

Find out what might interest you by talking to those in the know, says Beverly Bracker, director of career services at Thomas Jefferson School of Law in San Diego. Bracker recommends speaking with attorneys who are practicing in a particular area: Ask them about their day-to-day tasks and responsibilities, their greatest challenges, their most fulfilling and rewarding cases or transactions, and their advice to recent law grads. You can call lawyers and law firms for an informational interview, or you can opt to have your law school career services person do the work: Many of them keep lists of alumni who are willing to network and talk with students and recent grads about their career choices. "Lawyers will always talk," asserts Genevieve Bishop, associate director for employer relations at New York Law School. "They will tell you what their practice is like and also how they got there." Lawyers already working in an area can provide the best insight and tips for getting started—hence the reason for including their tips and advice in this book.

In addition to talking to others about different practice areas and career paths, do some serious thinking: Assess your own strengths, weaknesses, interests, and career goals. Some of this entails general career assessments, Bracker says—reading career books, taking self-assessment tests, and maybe even journaling through your job hunt. See Chapter 9 for a list of one hundred factors to consider when trying to find your niche.

Think broadly. Students have a surprisingly narrow focus when they get out, says Louis Thompson, assistant dean of career planning at Temple University Beasley School of Law. Thompson says it's hard to think of any employer who wouldn't want an employee with a JD—so think beyond the firm, even beyond the practice, if that's what interests you. "You need to open your eyes to the breadth of things you can do," agrees Bishop. But don't keep them open too long. "Some students get stuck in that phase," Bishop adds, which can take away from their focus on career options.

Don't base your career decisions strictly on your law school courses. "Pay attention to how you feel about the subject matter when you're taking the classes," Bishop says, but don't dismiss the subject if you didn't like it at first try. Look for practical experiences and real-world connections to help you make your career decisions. "Go and sit in on bar committees," recommends Bishop. "It's so inexpensive to join things as a student."

When it comes to résumés and cover letters, says Bishop, "I have seen students develop too much of a standardized approach." She recommends multiple résumés, each geared toward a different work environment or practice area. Bishop recalls one attorney who had trouble finding a corporate job; when Bishop looked at her résumé, she saw lots of impressive entries, but nothing that specifically showed an interest in in-house work. "Students have got to have what I [call] a coherent and integrated vision of themselves and the way their education, their limited practice experience, and their other activities fit together," Bishop says.

"Find some good mentors," says Bracker, "and not just one person, [but] different people at different stages in their careers. It's really important to have people you can go to with questions."

Practice everything—including the interview! Bracker says many students miss out when they fail to use their schools' career services office

127

for practice interviews. Even better, volunteer to do mock interviews on others, says Thompson. "You'll start honing your interview skills [and] seeing how other people interview."

If you're looking for a career change . . .
"Be calculating about the CLE seminars that you're attending," says Bracker. It's one way to start building a name for yourself. Also, become an expert at the practice area that you wish to go into: Research and write about topics, and get out there and start speaking to groups—whether it's the local Kiwanis Club or your homeowners' association, Bracker says—and develop a reputation for expertise in that practice area.

Recognize that shifting careers means shifting your outlook. "The biggest mistake is not recognizing that it's going to require a major mental shift," says Bishop. For example, Bishop says lawyers transitioning into a business environment sometimes have a hard time separating themselves from giving legal advice and don't want to take legal advice from other people, such as outside counsel. "Shifts are hard in terms of mentality," she says. "You have to appreciate the differences between what strengths each area of law and each environment is going to require of you."

"Understand not only what [your chosen] practice area is like, but what it's like in that segment," says Bishop. She says employers—whether legal or nonlegal—are looking for people who are practice-ready, business-ready, and culture-ready. Plus, while you're researching a new area or environment, you will also meet and interact with other people in the field, thereby making valuable connections.

When in doubt, just go for it. "Don't count yourself out," warns Ann Griffin, assistant dean of career services at Detroit Mercy, School of Law. Griffin says she's seen lawyers not go after jobs—particularly in alternative careers—because they didn't believe they would get them. "People actually don't pursue a lot of opportunities," agrees Thompson. "They self-select out of a lot of things; I'm always amazed at how many people don't even try."

And if you want to keep your career going . . .
You may coast by if you do all of the "right" things, but just as important to career success is knowing what actions you should avoid. There are some major pitfalls that can ruin your legal career. First, beware of burnout. "No matter whether you're changing careers or a student coming out of law school, you've got to keep some nonlegal interests," says Bishop. "You will not stay grounded if all you do is focus on your work,

even from the beginning. You've got to keep a sense of your place in the world outside of your practice."

Also beware of substance abuse and stress-related problems. According to a June 2005 article in the *ABA Journal*, as many as one in four lawyers experiences stress-related problems, and out of 105 professions, lawyers rank first in depression. In addition, substance abuse plays a part in a high number of bar disciplinary cases—some reports suggest as high as 70 percent. If you are struggling with stress, depression, or substance abuse, there is help and hope. Consult the ABA Commission on Lawyer Assistance Programs for information about a program in your area: http://www.abanet.org/legalservices/colap/.

Change your perception about building your network. Often, networking gets a bad rep—it conjures up images of fidgety law students telling corny jokes at awkward cocktail parties just to get noticed by the managing partner. But networking is not a one-size-fits-all situation. "Different atmospheres work for different people," says Bracker. "It isn't easy for most of us, [yet] we talk about it like it's the most natural thing to do," says Bishop. "I think networking becomes easier if you work on your personal professional ability to communicate with all kinds of people." Talking about jobs, even informally, can help you decide what you want to do and even lead to career opportunities, says Thompson—and it's often a good way to find out about unpublished job openings, adds Griffin. Listservs can also be a great networking tool (not to mention give you great insight into a practice area or environment), particularly for those who would rather communicate online.

Be mindful of personal guilt trips or regrets about your career. "You're not going to be happy all the time," says Griffin. "It's important to be realistic. Keep in mind that there are going to be some things on the negative side." Griffin says it's essential to keep "personal inventory" of your career and constantly evaluate whether the pros are still outweighing the cons—or whether it's time for a change. And if you're unhappy, go easy on yourself about past decisions. "That's the path you took and that's the only outcome you're going to know," Griffin says. "Give yourself the benefit of saying 'I did all the research possible and made the best choice [at the time].'"

It might seem like basic advice, but it's still important: Keep a sense of professionalism and courtesy. In the legal field, "everybody knows everybody, and word gets out when somebody does something inappropriate," says Bracker. Never underestimate the importance of your own personal reputation.

CHAPTER 9

Figuring Out What You WANT to Do

Landing a great position isn't easy, and landing the RIGHT position may be even tougher. As firms and other legal employers struggle with rising attrition rates, law graduates across the board struggle to find jobs that not only project the right image but also present the right fit. After all, everyone wants the perfect job.

No career book can decide for you the type of position that will be perfect for your needs, preferences, and goals. But by reading practitioners' descriptions of their careers in this book and then examining the following one hundred factors and deciding which ones are important to you—and which ones you can do without—you might have an easier time figuring it all out for yourself.

One Hundred Factors for Assessing Your Options

As you read through the one hundred factors (listed in no particular order) decide which ones matter to you. Write down the ten that you deem most important and the ten that are least important to you. Then, keep your list in mind as you consider applying for positions in various areas both within and outside of the legal profession.

I want to enjoy my work.

I want to work in a position where I have the power to help others.

I want to work on something new every day.

I want my job to challenge me.

I want a job that will use me to my fullest potential.
I want to learn something new every day.
I want to feel that I am helping my community in my work.
I want to perfect my skills in one specialty or practice area.
I want to work in various practice areas; I don't want to be pigeon-
holed.
I want to feel confident about my work product.
I want a satisfactory salary.
I want satisfactory fringe benefits.
I want to receive compensation that is fair in relation to that of my
peers.
I want a workplace that embraces merit-based compensation and
promotions.
I want job perks—from the company Blackberry to paid lunches.
I want to attain reasonable work-life balance, including time for my
family, personal pursuits, and hobbies.
I want manageable billable hour quotas.
I want manageable deadlines.
I want to have a flexible or alternative schedule.
I want to be able to work part-time if I choose.
I want to work in a field that offers assistance with student loan
repayment.
I want to work for an employer that doesn't pressure its attorneys to
bring in new business.
I want to work for an employer that encourages its attorneys to bring
in new business.
I want to work for an employer whose values match mine closely.
I want to work at a place where many different viewpoints and
values are represented.
I want to work with colleagues who have a strong work ethic.
I want to work in an environment that makes me feel comfortable
every day.
I want to work in an environment that frequently gets me out of my
comfort zone.
I want plenty of opportunities for advancement.
I want plenty of opportunities for professional development and
continuing education.
I want plenty of opportunities to perform pro bono work.
I want to work for an employer with low attrition rates.
I want to have access to cutting-edge legal technology and resources.
I want to have access to an advanced law library.

I want a pleasant work environment, up-to-date facilities, and positive working conditions.

I want to have access to help by support staff.

I want to work with a diverse group.

I want to work with people who are a lot like me.

I want to work for an employer who values cultural sensitivity and diversity in the workplace.

I want to be in court a lot.

I want to write a lot.

I want to research a lot.

I want to have lots of client contact.

I want to enjoy working with the clients I serve.

I want to negotiate with others.

I want to help others resolve their controversies.

I want the opportunity to attend plenty of networking functions.

I want to work for an employer that provides opportunities for socializing with colleagues outside of work.

I want to work for a large firm.

I want to work for a small firm.

I want to work for the government.

I want to work for a nonprofit organization.

I want to work in education or academia.

I want to be my own boss.

I want recognition for my contributions at work.

I want to be busy at work.

I want to feel productive at all times.

I don't want to feel overwhelmed by the amount of work I am given.

I want to practice law.

I don't want to practice law.

I want to practice law in nontraditional ways.

I want to have the opportunity to train or teach others in my areas of expertise.

I want to be given authority over my own cases.

I want to be given substantive and meaningful work assignments.

I want the opportunity to travel for work.

I want the opportunity to work with people from other countries or cultures.

I want to be involved in the day-to-day operations and management of my workplace.

I want my own office.

I want to have periodic evaluations and frequent feedback.

I want to have clearly defined and explained performance goals set for me by my workplace.

I want firmly defined company policies in place, communicated clearly to me and other employees.

I want to know that I have supervisors to whom I can turn with questions.

I don't want to be micromanaged.

I want access to formal and informal mentoring on the job.

I want a workplace with an open door policy, where my supervisors and colleagues are approachable.

I want a workplace where the channels of communication are open.

I want to work with partners or senior-level staff as closely as possible.

I want to have collegial respect for my coworkers, including my supervisors.

I want to experience collegial respect from my coworkers, including my supervisors.

I want to make friends with my coworkers.

I want to be left alone to work independently.

I want a workplace where office politics are kept to a minimum.

I want to have colleagues who exhibit a high level of professionalism.

I want to work for an employer who has a positive reputation in the legal and business communities.

I want to work for an employer who has an international presence.

I want a workplace that is loyal to its employees, whose employees likewise exhibit loyalty to the firm.

I want a workplace that is well managed.

I want a workplace with a proven record of profitability.

I want to work for a prestigious employer.

I want a workplace that pays attention to marketing its attorneys and legal services.

I want to build a skill set that will readily translate into a variety of career options in the future.

I want to work in a position that will ultimately advance not only my skill set but also my long-term career goals.

I want an entry-level position that I hope to hold just for the next few years.

I want a long-term position.

I want a manageable commute.

I want to share in the profits that my employer derives from my work.

I want job security.

I want to participate in important decisions that happen in my workplace.

I want to work for an employer who's amenable to organizational change and growth.

I want to feel proud of the work I do.

INDEX

ABOUT THE AUTHOR

Ursula Furi-Perry, JD, is a nationally published legal writer, attorney, and adjunct professor with more than three hundred articles to her credit. She pens the career column for the *National Jurist*, as well as the recent law grad profile column for both the *Jurist* and its sister publication, *preLaw*. Her writing has been published by Law.com, American Lawyer Media, the American Bar Association, LawCrossing.com, *Legal Assistant Today*, and several of the *Boston Herald*'s community publications. She writes the Legally Mom Blog at http://www.wickedlocalparents.com/legallymom/.

Her first book, *50 Legal Careers for Nonlawyers*, was published in 2008 by American Bar Association Publishing and is available at the ABA store online at http://www.abanet.org/abastore/index.cfm.

Furi-Perry is an adjunct professor of writing and legal reasoning at the Massachusetts School of Law at Andover. She also teaches paralegal courses at Bridgewater State College in Bridgewater, Massachusetts, and Northern Essex Community College in Lawrence, Massachusetts.

Furi-Perry received her juris doctorate from the Massachusetts School of Law and graduated magna cum laude from her law school class. Visit her website at www.furiperry.com.